Dominoes

THE LAST OF THE MOHICANS

Great Clarendon Street, Oxford OX2 6DP

Oxford University Press is a department of the University of Oxford.
It furthers the University's objective of excellence in research, scholarship,
and education by publishing worldwide in

Oxford New York

Auckland Bangkok Buenos Aires Cape Town Chennai
Dar es Salaam Delhi Hong Kong Istanbul Karachi Kolkata
Kuala Lumpur Madrid Melbourne Mexico City Mumbai
Nairobi São Paulo Shanghai Taipei Tokyo Toronto

OXFORD and OXFORD ENGLISH are registered trade marks of
Oxford University Press in the UK and in certain other countries

The moral rights of the author have been asserted

Database right Oxford University Press (maker)

First published 2003
2008 2007 2006 2005 2004
10 9 8 7 6 5 4 3 2

ISBN 0 19 424403 2

A complete recording of this Dominoes edition of
The Last of the Mohicans is available on cassette ISBN 0 19 424387 7

Printed in Hong Kong

ACKNOWLEDGEMENTS

The publisher would like to thank the following for permission to reproduce photographs: Corbis pp 13 (canoe/Edward S Curtis/© Stapleton Collection), 37 (A Native Ojibwa American poses as Hiawatha/© Hulton-Deutsch Collection), 53 (Flathead Chief), 60 (tomahawk/© Bettmann), 70 (totem pole/Gunter Marx Photography); DK Images p 74 (cat washing/Jane Burton); NHPA pp74 (dingo/Martin Harvey, snake/ Daniel Heuclin, bobcat/T Kitchin & V Hurst, bear/Andy Rouse); OUP collection pp 44, 71 (background leaves) 74 (deer); Powerstock p 74 (birds/John W Warden, tortoise/© Morales); Stone p 76 (black cat/G. K & Vicky Hart); Taxi p 76 (boy and cat/ Marina Jefferson).

The publishers have made every effort to contact the copyright holder of the film still on the front cover, but have been unable to do so. If the copyright holders would like to contact the publishers, the publishers would be happy to pay an appropriate reproduction fee.

Dominoes

SERIES EDITORS: BILL BOWLER AND SUE PARMINTER

THE LAST OF THE MOHICANS

JAMES FENIMORE COOPER

Text adaptation by Bill Bowler

Illustrated by Thomas Sperling

LEVEL THREE ■ 1,000 HEADWORDS

James Fenimore Cooper (1789–1851) grew up near Lake Otsego in the State of New York. His father was a rich man, and Cooper was sent to study at Yale College. Cooper was not a good student and he was expelled in his third year at college, so he joined the Navy and went to sea. Later, after his father's death, he returned home to live a comfortable life as a gentleman farmer. It was only when his father's fortune ran out, that Cooper, at the age of thirty, started writing. He wrote many books, but his best-known work is *The Last of the Mohicans* (1826). It is the second book in a series of five adventure stories describing the life of early settlers in America.

OXFORD

UNIVERSITY PRESS

BEFORE READING

1 *The Last of the Mohicans* takes place in North America in 1757. Here are some of the characters in the story.

1 Cora and Alice

2 Duncan Heyward

3 Magua

4 David Gamut

5 Uncas

6 Hawk-eye

Match these sentences with the pictures.

a ☐ He's an Indian from the Mohican tribe. They're friendly with the British.
b ☐ He's an Indian from the Huron tribe. They're not friendly with the British.
c ☐ He can shoot with a gun very well. He knows the Indians very well too.
d ☐ They're sisters. They want to visit their father, General Munro.
e ☐ He's from England. He's a singing teacher and he likes going to church.
f ☐ He's an officer in the British army. He's fighting the French. He's in love with Alice.

2 Think about the title of this book. What will happen to Uncas? What problems do you think Indian tribes had in those days?

CHAPTER 1

THE INDIAN GUIDE

When North America still belonged to both Great Britain and France, there was **war** between their two armies. The land between the head of the Hudson River and the nearby lakes saw some **fierce** fighting. Lake Champlain started in French Canada and ended in British land, where it was joined by Lake Horican. From Lake Horican it was a journey of only a few miles over land to the Hudson River and from there you could sail to the sea. So the French were interested in winning this land, and the British wanted to keep it. Important battles were fought here, and many **forts** were built here too.

Our story begins in the third year of this war. One day in the middle of the summer, a fierce-looking Indian **runner** arrived at Fort Edward, the British fort at the south of the land route that went from Lake Horican to the Hudson River. He brought news that the French **General**, Montcalm, was crossing Lake Champlain with a **huge** army. He also brought a message from General Munro, the old Scottish officer **commanding** Fort William Henry, which stood on Lake Horican, asking for **reinforcements** to help him to fight against Montcalm.

General Webb, the commander of Fort Edward, had 5,000 soldiers under him, and he decided to send 1,500 men as reinforcements to General Munro the next day. Early the next morning the soldiers marched north out of the fort, travelling along the wide army road towards Fort William Henry.

That same day, another, smaller, group of people was also getting ready to travel to Fort William Henry. There were three fine horses waiting outside General Webb's house, and a small crowd of people stood watching them. Among this crowd was a very strange person. He was tall and thin, with

war fighting between the armies of two or more countries

fierce strong, hard and frightening

fort a safe place for soldiers to live in with high and strong walls around it

runner a person who takes messages from one place to another

general a very important army officer

huge very big

command to be the most important person and tell others what to do

reinforcements extra men who are sent to make an army stronger

a large head and huge feet. He wore a sky-blue coat, yellow trousers tied at the knee, white cotton **stockings** and shoes, an old, dirty shirt, and a large black hat.

While he watched, three figures left General Webb's house. A young officer was followed by two young women dressed in fine travelling clothes. The younger of the two was fair, with blue eyes. She smiled at the officer as he helped her onto her horse. The other woman, whom the officer also helped onto her horse, was beautiful too, but a little older. She wore a green **scarf** and had fine black hair and dark eyes. It was hard to think that the two women were sisters; one was so fair and the other was so much darker.

Finally the officer climbed onto his own horse and the three rode off, following the Indian runner. As they left, the fair-haired woman **pointed** at the Indian and began to talk to the officer riding at her side.

'Are there many men like him in the forests here, Duncan?' she asked **Major** Heyward. 'He's a little frightening.'

'Don't worry, Alice. Magua's just an army runner. He's promised to be our **guide** and to take us to Fort William Henry by a shorter, secret **path** through the forest.'

'I don't like the look of him, Duncan,' replied Alice. 'But I suppose that if you know him he must be all right.'

'Well, I know that he used to be on the side of the French. In fact I **believe** your father punished him some years ago, although I don't remember much about it. But now he's a friend of the British, and that's good enough for me.'

'My father's enemy in the past?' said Alice. 'I like him even less.'

At that point the Indian runner stopped and pointed to a narrow path that disappeared into the forest.

'Here's our path,' said Major Heyward.

'What do you think, Cora?' asked Alice, 'Shall we travel on slowly but safely with the army or go this way on our own?'

stockings thin clothes that you wear on the lower part of your legs

scarf something that you wear around your neck

point to show something with your finger

major an army officer

guide someone who shows other people where to go

path a narrow road for people to walk on

believe to think that something is true

'Alice we won't be safer with the army,' said Heyward. 'If we go with them, our enemies will know where to find us easily. This secret route will be much quicker and safer.'

'Can we not **trust** a man with dark skin, Alice?' added Cora, coldly.

So they left the wide road and entered the forest, following the Indian guide. They had not gone far before they heard something crashing through the forest behind them, getting closer. They turned and waited until at last they could see what was making all the noise. The strange man in the blue coat, yellow trousers and white stockings **appeared**, riding a young horse towards them. Heyward smiled, and Alice and Cora were also amused to see him.

'Are you looking for someone?' asked Heyward.

'Yes,' replied the stranger. 'My name is David Gamut. I am a singing teacher. I hear you are travelling to Fort William Henry and I'd like to come with you.'

'The road is there, behind you, sir,' replied Heyward.

'Oh, Duncan, please let him come with us,' said Alice to Heyward, and she looked at Cora and the Indian guide who was standing close by her. 'Perhaps we'll need him later.'

trust to believe that someone is honest and good

appear to be suddenly in front of someone's eyes

bush a small low tree

fire-water an Indian name for whiskey

tribe a large family of Indians

'Very well,' replied the major, and he rode over to Cora.

All four riders now turned and followed their Indian guide through the trees. David Gamut sang as they went. Not one of them realized that there were Indians hiding behind **bushes** in the forest, watching their every step

At a river's edge, two men were talking. One was an Indian, the other a white man whose skin was dark from the sun, and who was wearing clothes made from animal skins.

'Tell me about the old times, Chingachgook,' said the white man.

'Hawk-eye, my friend. We were happy before the white man came here. The lake gave us fish, the sky gave us birds, and the forest gave us animals to eat. Then the Dutch came and gave our people **fire-water** to drink, and we gave our lands to them. Slowly the white men killed us one by one. Now our **tribe** has nearly gone. Only I and my son Uncas are left. And when I die, Uncas will be the last of the Mohicans.'

Out of the forest another, younger Indian came to join them.

'Father,' he said. 'I come from the forest where the Hurons are hiding. There are white men riding this way.'

'They are your brothers, Hawk-eye. You should speak to them,' said Chingachgook to the white man.

At that moment Heyward rode out of the forest at the

river's edge. Cora, Alice, Gamut and their Indian guide were some fifty steps behind him.

'Who goes there?' called Hawk-eye picking up his **rifle**.

'Friends of the British King,' replied Heyward. 'Are we on the right path for Fort William Henry?'

'The right path?' laughed Hawk-eye. 'The wrong path is what you mean. The road to William Henry is behind you.'

'Yes, but our Indian guide was taking us on a secret path through the forest. He got lost, so I put him at the back.'

'A lost Indian?' said Hawk-eye. 'I can't believe that, although it's true that you're going the wrong way. Where's he from?'

'He's a Huron from the north, but friendly to the British.'

Chingachgook and Uncas jumped up at these words.

'Never trust a Huron,' said Hawk-eye. 'I don't mind who his friends are. I'm surprised that you haven't had more trouble from him. There are more Hurons hiding in this forest, you know. But wait a moment. Chingachgook and Uncas will catch him and then we can question him.'

Silently Hawk-eye's Indian friends disappeared into the bushes. A moment later, Cora, Alice, and Gamut rode from between the trees to join Hawk-eye and Heyward, while Magua stopped at the edge of the forest. Heyward got off his horse and went over to speak to him.

'Why did we come this way, Magua? We're lost! This Englishman here tells me that you are a very bad guide!'

'Then Magua will leave you here in the forest!'

'But what will the Scottish chief of Fort William Henry say then? He will be very angry to hear that Magua left his daughters with no guide.'

Suddenly there was a noise of a breaking branch and, like a frightened animal, Magua ran off into the forest. Uncas and Chingachgook jumped from the bushes and chased him, and Hawk-eye lifted his rifle to his shoulder and shot after him – but Magua had already disappeared into the trees.

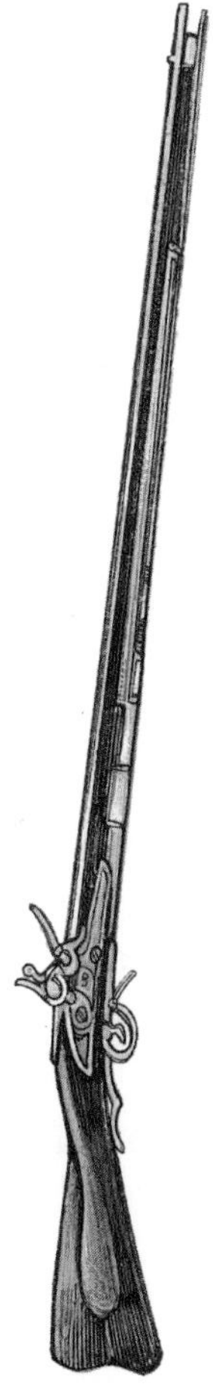

rifle a long gun

READING CHECK

Choose the right words to complete the sentences.

a The story begins when . . .

1 ☑ the French want to win some British land in North America.

2 ☐ the British want to win some French land in North America.

3 ☐ the Indians want to win back some of their land in North America.

b Cora and Alice . . .

1 ☐ are going to meet their father at Fort William Henry.

2 ☐ decide to travel with the British army.

3 ☐ are both happy to follow Magua.

c David Gamut, the singing teacher, . . .

1 ☐ is travelling with Cora and Alice.

2 ☐ follows Cora and Alice into the forest.

3 ☐ wants to help Cora and Alice find Fort William Henry.

d Uncas and Chingachgook . . .

1 ☐ are friends of the Huron Indians.

2 ☐ are the last two Mohicans.

3 ☐ show Cora, Alice and Heyward the way to Fort William Henry.

e Hawk-eye . . .

1 ☐ doesn't think Mohicans are honest.

2 ☐ kills Magua.

3 ☐ is dressed like an Indian.

WORD WORK

1 Match the words with the correct definitions.

bush fort general guide path scarf stocking

a this person is the head of an army

b this is a strong building used in a war

c you can travel over land by walking along this

d this plant is like a small, low tree

e something you wear to cover your neck or your head

f something you wear on your foot and leg

g this person shows you the way to go

2 Find words in the leaves to complete the sentences.

a There is f_i_e_r_c_e fighting between the British and French in North America.

b Cora and Alice's father c_ _ _ _ _ _ _ _ Fort William Henry on Lake Horican.

c Montcalm has a h_ _ _ army.

d Munro asks Webb to send r_ _ _ _ _ _ _ _ _ _ _ _ _ to Fort William Henry.

e Duncan Heyward is a m_ _ _ _ in the British army.

f Magua p_ _ _ _ _ to a narrow path going into the forest.

g Indians from the Huron t_ _ _ _ were usually more friendly with the French than with the British.

h Alice doesn't t_ _ _ _ Magua.

i Heyward b_ _ _ _ _ _ _ that Magua is a friend of the British.

ierec

sdamnom

egu

neicerfotnesm

orja

sonit

rieb

ruts

sleivee

GUESS WHAT

What happens in the next chapter? Tick two boxes.

a ☐ Hawk-eye and Heyward catch Magua.

b ☐ Hawk-eye and the Mohicans take the others to a secret hiding place.

c ☐ Uncas and Chingachgook help them to find the path to Fort William Henry.

d ☐ The Hurons attack Heyward and the others.

e ☐ Cora and Alice safely arrive at Fort William Henry.

f ☐ They all decide to return to Fort Edward.

CHAPTER 2

BEHIND THE WATERFALL

Seeing Hawk-eye run after Magua, Heyward also began to chase him, but soon he met the white **scout**, together with Chingachgook and Uncas, walking back through the forest.

'Did you find him?' asked Heyward.

'How can a cloud catch the wind?' replied Hawk-eye. 'I shot him, at least,' he went on, pointing to the blood on the ground.

'Shall we go after him?' asked Heyward.

'And let him **lead** us to the Hurons, or to Montcalm?' asked Hawk-eye. 'No. We should leave this place at once. And let us cover our **tracks**, so the Hurons cannot follow us.'

'I'll pay you well to take us to Fort William Henry,' said Heyward.

Hawk-eye and his two Indian friends talked together in low voices in Mohican. At last Hawk-eye turned to Heyward.

'Keep your money. The Mohicans and I will help you and the two young ladies to escape to safety. We want no money, but you must promise two things – the first is to keep as still and silent as the forest, and the second is never to tell another living person the way to our hiding place.'

'Agreed,' said Heyward, and he went to explain the plan to Cora and Alice.

'What can we do with the horses?' Hawk-eye asked himself. 'We can't let them go free, or the Hurons will find them and know that we're near. Three of the horses are old and will keep quiet if they must – so we can take them with us. But the singing teacher's horse is young and noisy – we will have to kill it and throw it into the river.'

He turned to Uncas. 'Take that young horse—' he began.

scout someone who goes in front of other people to find a path through wild country

lead (*past* **led**) to go in front for others to follow

tracks these are left on the ground by people or animals travelling across it

'Stop!' cried Gamut, 'Keep your hands off my horse!'

'Listen,' explained Hawk-eye. 'All our lives are in danger. If you want your horse to live, we'll leave you here for the Hurons. Or think again and let Uncas do what has to be done.'

Gamut fell silent and Uncas and Chingachgook killed the young horse. They then led the other horses into the river, and began to walk up it, against the **current**. From a hiding place under some bushes Hawk-eye pulled a **canoe**, and Alice and Cora sat in it. With Heyward standing in the water on one side of the boat and Hawk-eye on the other, they moved after Gamut, who followed the Mohicans. After some time they reached a lonely place where high walls of rock, with trees on top, stood tall and wild on either side of the running water. In front of them was another high rock wall with **caves** in it. Down this ran a noisy waterfall.

In this narrow valley the Mohicans left their horses tied to some bushes at the edge of the water. At the same time Hawk-eye, Heyward and Gamut got into the canoe with Cora and Alice. Then Hawk-eye

current the way the water moves in a river

canoe a long, narrow, light Indian boat

cave a big hole in the side of a hill

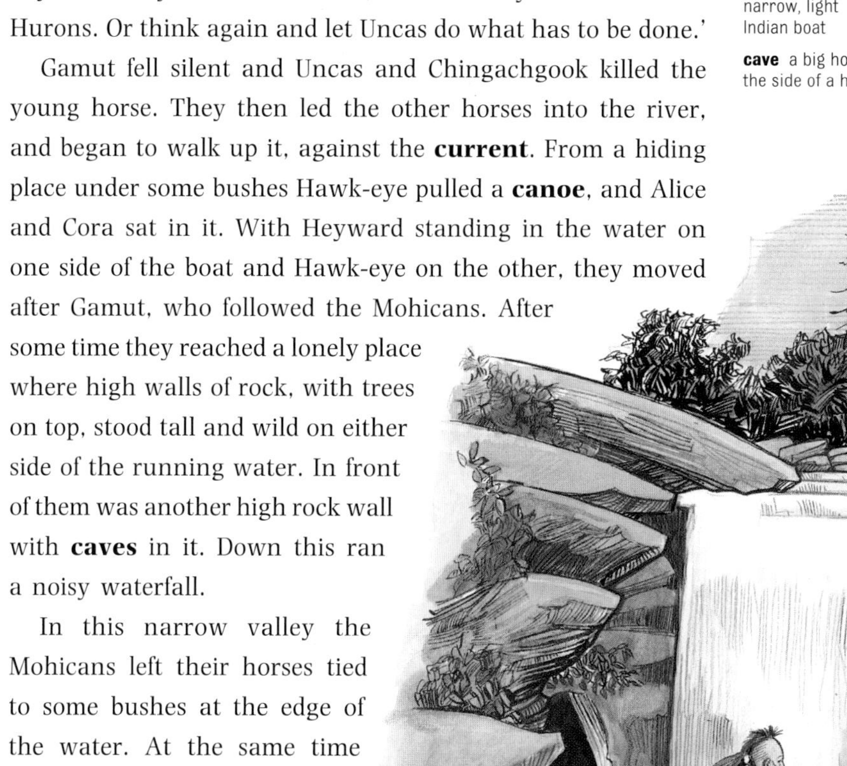

steered the little boat straight towards the waterfall. After trying several times, at last the canoe landed in still water by a flat rock at the centre of the waterfall.

'Here we are, at Glenn's Waterfall,' said Hawk-eye.

Heyward, Cora, Alice and Gamut got out of the canoe and waited on the rock while Hawk-eye steered it back to get Uncas and Chingachgook. Soon they returned, and took the food and blankets, which they had brought with them, from the bottom of the canoe.

After that, the Mohicans and the white scout disappeared into a cave in the rock and the others followed. Soon a fire was burning and the smell of cooking meat filled the air.

'Uncas,' said Hawk-eye. 'Put two blankets up to cover both entrances of the cave. We don't want the Hurons to see the light of our fire. And now,' he went on, turning to the others. 'Sit and eat. There's salt to add taste if you need it.'

After supper, Gamut and the ladies sang. Then they suddenly heard a ghostly cry from outside the cave. What was it? The men went outside into the night to listen.

'I think it's the horses!' said Heyward, as the cry came again. 'Something's frightening them. But is it Hurons or **wolves**?'

'Well at least the cry is no longer a mystery,' said Hawk-eye. 'And now I think we men should watch while the young ladies sleep for a while.'

Cora and Alice slept in the cave. At one entrance sat the Mohicans and Hawk-eye. Heyward and Gamut sat at the other, and were soon asleep.

At the first light of day, Hawk-eye woke them quietly. Heyward went at once to get Cora and Alice. Suddenly they heard cries from outside. From the far side of the river, Huron rifles shot at Gamut where he stood at the cave mouth, and he fell to the ground, hitting his head on a rock. Heyward quickly ran and pulled him into the cave, while Hawk-eye

steer to move a boat to left or right

wolf (*plural* **wolves**) a big grey animal like a dog that lives in the wild

shot and killed one of the Huron gunmen.

Cora looked at Gamut, lying white-faced and still on the floor of the cave. 'Is he dead?' she whispered.

'No, he was lucky. But he needs to rest,' said Hawk-eye.

He and Heyward took their rifles and hid in some bushes at the water's edge. After some time they noticed a Huron at the top of the waterfall above them. Before their eyes the current pulled him to his death in the river below.

Then four more Hurons appeared and climbed down from the top of the waterfall towards them. Hawk-eye's rifle killed the first. Then Uncas came out of the cave to help them. He killed one Huron and came to help Heyward, who was **wrestling** with another at the edge of the waterfall. Moving quickly, Uncas cut the wrist of Heyward's enemy, and he fell back into the white water and was pulled under. Hawk-eye killed his man with a knife through the heart.

Then, from a tree at the top of the wall of rock on the other side of the river, a Huron fighter began shooting down at them. They lay low in the bushes and waited. At last Hawk-eye managed to shoot up into the tree and the Huron fell to his death on the rocks in the river below.

'My last bullet!' said the scout. 'Let's fetch more from the canoe.'

But they found that the Hurons had cut the **ropes** and stolen the canoe. They went back to the cave to talk.

'What can we do now?' asked Heyward.

'Nothing,' replied Hawk-eye. 'We are dead men.'

'No,' said Cora, 'You mustn't die. You must leave us here and go to Fort William Henry!'

'And what shall we say to your father?' asked Hawk-eye.

'Tell him to come at once with an army to save us.'

A few minutes later, Hawk-eye, Chingachgook and Uncas dropped into the river and swam off, leaving Cora, Alice, Heyward and the sleeping Gamut in the cave.

wrestle to fight with your hands

rope a long, thick string

READING CHECK

Put these sentences in the correct order. Number them 1-9.

a ☐ Hawk-eye, Heyward, and the Mohicans fight the Hurons.
b [1] Hawk-eye decides to let Magua escape.
c ☐ Hawk-eye and the Mohicans agree to take them to Fort William Henry.
d ☐ Hawk-eye finds that he has no more bullets.
e ☐ The Mohicans lead the others up the river to a waterfall.
f ☐ Uncas and Chingachgook kill Gamut's horse.
g ☐ They reach their secret hiding place in a cave behind a waterfall.
h ☐ Hawk-eye and the Mohicans leave Cora, Alice, Gamut, and Heyward in the cave.
i ☐ The Hurons attack the cave and hurt Gamut.

WORD WORK

Use the words in the waterfall to complete the sentences on page 13.

canoe
caves
~~current~~
lead
rope
scouts
steer
tracks
wolves
wrestled

a When you're on a river with a fast current, it isn't easy to .... a small boat like a ....

b Indians are excellent .... They are very good at finding, understanding and following .... on the ground.

c .... are like wild dogs.

d .... are where people lived thousands of years ago. They are warm in the winter and cool in the summer.

e You .... us along the right path and we'll follow you.

f They tied her hands together with a ....

g Instead of fighting with guns or knives, they .... on the ground.

GUESS WHAT

What happens in the next chapter? Tick the boxes.

Who . . .	**Heyward**	**Magua**	**David Gamut**
a . . . asks Cora to marry him?			
b . . . starts singing?			
c . . . makes a hiding place in the cave?			
d . . . talks to Magua?			
e . . . fights Magua?			
f . . . is angry with Cora's father?			

CHAPTER 3

MAGUA'S PLANS

Now that Hawk-eye and the Mohicans had swum off, Heyward looked around him. For the moment everything was calm.

Gamut came out of the cave, holding his aching head. He was still feeling **weak** from the bad knock he had when he fell against the rock.

'What's happening?' he asked.

'The Hurons have gone, for a while at least,' replied Heyward. 'Let's hide in the cave and hope that they don't find us.'

So the soldier and the singing teacher went into the cave. Cora sat there bravely, but Alice was crying.

'Alice,' said Heyward. 'We are alive, and with life there's hope.'

'Yes,' replied Alice, looking up at him. 'And all my hopes are with those brave men who are going to fetch our father.'

Heyward then took some branches and put them one on top of the other to hide the **passage** that joined the larger and smaller parts of the cave. Using Hawk-eye's blankets he filled the holes between the branches, and soon their part of the cave was dark, lit only by the weak light that came through the narrow second entrance at the side of the cave.

Taking his gun and his last few bullets in his hand, he turned with a **grim** face to watch the narrow cave entrance.

'The Hurons won't find us easy to **capture**,' he said to himself.

'Well, now, shall we sing a little?' said Gamut bravely. He took a little song book out of his pocket and began to sing.

'Isn't singing dangerous with the Hurons so close?' Cora asked.

'Poor man,' replied Heyward, 'his voice is so weak. I honestly don't think that the Hurons will hear it.'

weak not strong

passage a long narrow way between two caves

grim very serious

capture to take someone or something as a prisoner

But only a short while later David Gamut's song was **interrupted** by a Huron cry just outside the **main** entrance to the cave. All eyes turned to the thin wall of branches and blankets that stood between them and their enemies. Heyward lifted up the corner of a blanket to see what was happening in the main part of the cave.

The Hurons were there. One man held Hawk-eye's useless rifle, and they seemed to be looking for the white scout everywhere. But, apart from seeing some of David Gamut's blood on the cave floor, which excited them greatly, they found nothing of interest to them.

Heyward, Gamut, and the two Munro sisters kept silent and hoped that the Hurons wouldn't discover their secret hiding place behind the branches. At last the Huron fighters left the main cave and their cries grew fainter as they went off to explore the rest of the rocky island.

Heyward turned to his friends. 'They've gone!' he said.

Alice opened her mouth to say something, but suddenly her eyes widened and she screamed.

Heyward turned to look at the side entrance of the cave. There, against the light, he saw the dark figure of Magua.

Without thinking, he shot at the man, but Magua ran off to safety, and the noise of the gun immediately brought the Hurons back to the cave. The wall of branches and blankets was quickly pulled to pieces, and Heyward, the Munro sisters, and Gamut were led out into the daylight.

The Hurons stood all around them, angrily shouting at them in French and sometimes talking together in their own language. One of them – a tall, strong man – seemed, in Heyward's eyes, to be their chief. He called Magua to him and spoke to him for a few minutes. Then Magua came over to the prisoners and explained what the others were saying.

'They are looking for the white scout "Long-rifle",' he said, using the Indians' name for Hawk-eye, 'and his Mohican friends,

interrupt to stop something in the middle

main most important

attack to start fighting

bank the land at the side of a river or lake

tomahawk a small wood and metal thing that you hold in your hands and use to throw or to fight with

Chingachgook and Uncas. Where are they?'

'They swam off down the river,' replied Heyward with a grim smile. 'You'll never catch them now.'

Magua explained Heyward's words to the other Hurons, who looked angry. Then the Huron chief spoke. From time to time he pointed towards Fort Edward, and Heyward felt sure he was worried that General Webb would **attack** them.

After the chief had finished, Heyward, Gamut and the women were marched to the river **bank**, where a canoe was waiting. They got in and two Hurons got in after them. In moments the current took them back to the place where they had entered the river with Hawk-eye and the Mohicans the day before.

They got out on the other bank. Soon the Huron chief arrived on Heyward's horse, followed by the rest of the Hurons and the other horses. They left Magua and five other Indians with the prisoners, and rode off towards Fort William Henry. Heyward spoke to Magua who was standing under a tree.

'You were clever to pretend to join the French although you are a still a true friend of the British. But when will you get rid of these others and lead us to General Munro? He will give you many presents for bringing his daughters to him.'

'Send the dark-haired woman here to speak to me,' replied Magua playing with a small **tomahawk** in his hand.

Heyward led Cora to him. Like Alice and Gamut, her wrists

were now tied with rope. Instead of leaving Cora and Magua alone, Heyward stood not far off, watching. Another Huron came to stand at Magua's side.

'What do you wish to say, Magua?' Cora asked their **former** guide.

'Only this. Your father had me beaten one day for drinking fire-water and I cannot forget that. I was a chief among my people before I came to live here and you do not beat a chief.' He looked down at his tomahawk.

'And why are you telling me this?' asked Cora.

'Because you can help your sister and your friends. I will take them to your father if you promise me something.'

'What?' asked Cora, her blood running cold.

'You will become my wife. You will live with me. You will sleep in my bed and cook my food for me. Then General Munro will not make war against my people again, because my knife will never be far from his daughter's neck.'

Cora looked at him angrily. 'Never!' she cried.

At that, Magua threw his tomahawk angrily at the tree just beyond where Cora stood, and the Indian at his side pulled out his knife. But before he could use it on Cora, Heyward ran between them and wrestled him to the ground. The Indian was stronger than the young soldier and soon he was on top and winning the fight. He lifted his knife in the air, hoping to **drive** it down into Heyward's heart. Then suddenly there was a rifle shot, and the Huron fell dead at Heyward's side.

former in the past

drive (*past* **drove**, **driven**) to push very hard

READING CHECK

Match the first and second parts of these sentences.

- **a** Heyward makes a wall . . .
- **b** Gamut sings . . .
- **c** The Hurons come through the main entrance . . .
- **d** Alice, Cora, Heyward, and Gamut . . .
- **e** Magua comes . . .
- **f** The Hurons come back to the cave . . .
- **g** The Hurons take their prisoners . . .
- **h** Heyward tells Magua that Munro will . . .
- **i** Magua says that he wants Cora to marry him . . .

1. to make himself feel braver.
2. give him presents for saving his daughters.
3. hide quietly behind the wall of branches
4. and search the main cave.
5. because he hates her father.
6. into the cave through the side entrance.
7. of branches and blankets in the cave.
8. when they hear Heyward's shot.
9. back down the river again.

WORD WORK

Correct the boxed words in these sentences.
All the words come from Chapter 3.

- **a** It wasn't easy for them to **rapture** Heyward. capture.
- **b** The **pain** entrance to the cave was big. ....
- **c** He was fishing on the river **band**. ....
- **d** A short **massage** joined one cave and the next cave. ....
- **e** She took a knife and **prove** it into his chest. ....
- **f** He didn't smile. His face was **gram**. ....
- **g** Later the Hurons **attached** the cave. ....
- **h** I felt very **wear** after being so ill. ....
- **i** He couldn't finish speaking because she **interested** him angrily. ....
- **j** In **farmer** times he worked for Munro. ....

GUESS WHAT

What happens in the next chapter? Tick the boxes.

a 1 ☐ 2 ☐ . . . fights with Magua.

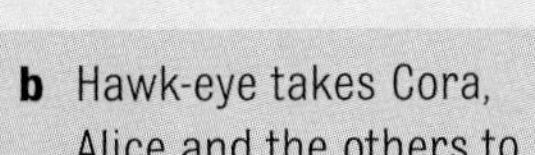

b Hawk-eye takes Cora, Alice and the others to . . . 1 ☐ 2 ☐ . . for the night.

c In the end, they reach . . . 1 ☐ 2 ☐ . . . safely.

CHAPTER 4

SAFE AGAIN

It **shocked** Magua and the other Hurons to see one of their number die so suddenly. There were cries of 'Long-rifle'. The dead man was wrestling with Heyward when he was shot. Hawk-eye was the only gunman they knew who could safely shoot one wrestling man and miss the other. Almost immediately, Hawk-eye appeared with his rifle from behind some bushes, together with Uncas, who was holding his tomahawk. Chingachgook also came forward, and ran towards Cora. Hawk-eye hurried forwards, not stopping to put fresh bullets in his rifle but using it to beat his enemies.

Magua picked up a knife and ran to meet Chingachgook, and the three other Hurons got ready to fight Hawk-eye and Uncas. Heyward pulled Magua's tomahawk from the tree and ran to join them. Now it was Magua and his three friends against Heyward and his three.

Heyward threw Magua's tomahawk at one of the Hurons. It hit the Indian on the head and this stopped him for a while, but when Heyward ran forward and began to wrestle with him, he realized that the man was not badly hurt and was still fighting strongly. He was saved by Hawk-eye who brought his rifle down hard on the Huron's head and killed him.

Uncas, who had just killed another Huron fighter with his tomahawk, now ran to help Cora, who had untied the rope around her wrists and was trying to untie Alice. From behind them, a Huron quickly caught the older sister by the hair and pushed her to the ground, lifting his knife in the air to kill her. But Uncas jumped on him, and Heyward and Hawk-eye were not far behind. Soon the Huron lay dead at Cora's feet.

Now Heyward, Hawk-eye, and Uncas ran back to see the

shock to give someone a very bad surprise

fight between Chingachgook and Magua.

The two figures wrestled fiercely on the ground at the edge of a **slope**, their knives bright in the sunlight. And Heyward, Hawk-eye, and Uncas looked on, unable to help for fear of hurting Chingachgook.

Then, suddenly, Chingachgook drove his knife forward and Magua fell back, still and silent. At last he was dead, it seemed. Chingachgook began to dance and sing a song of **victory**.

Hawk-eye lifted his rifle in the air in order to bring it down hard on Magua's head. But before he could do anything, the Huron suddenly came to life, **rolled** down the slope, and ran off to safety in the forest.

'What a dishonest man!' said Hawk-eye. 'He couldn't even die bravely. Well, let him go. He has no knife, and he's far from his French friends. He's no danger to us now.'

Cora untied Alice's wrists and Hawk-eye did the same

slope a place where the land goes down; the side of a hill

victory winning a fight

roll to move by turning over and over

with David Gamut. They found Cora's and Alice's horses tied to trees at the foot of the slope, together with some **deer** meat that the Hurons had caught, ready to eat. There was a **spring** nearby so they all stopped for a drink. Then Uncas found wood, made a fire, and began to cook the meat, and at the same time Hawk-eye told Heyward of their adventures.

'We had no time to reach the fort and return to save you. So instead we hid in the forest, followed your tracks, and waited until the right moment to attack.'

After they had drunk some water, eaten some meat, and rested, the two sisters got on their horses, and with Hawk-eye, Heyward, Gamut, and the Mohicans walking at their side, they moved off towards Fort William Henry.

Towards late evening, they reached a number of tall trees that stood in a circle. Thick bushes grew between them.

'If I remember rightly, there's an old wooden house in the middle of those trees,' said Hawk-eye. 'It's a place where we can rest for a while safe from attack. Then, when the moon is in the sky, we must travel on.'

So the group of travellers passed between the trees and up the hill which stood beyond them. The roof of the house had fallen in, but Hawk-eye, Uncas, and Chingachgook entered the walls and looked around with interest. Heyward, Gamut, and the Munro sisters followed them.

'Chingachgook and I built this house years ago to be safe from attack during a war between the Mohicans and another tribe,' went on Hawk-eye. 'I fought here, and of all the Mohicans who built this house, he and I were the only men alive at the end of the fight. The dead lie under the grass outside.'

Some stones marked the place where the dead men lay, and Cora and Alice looked at the place sadly. Then they all drank from an old spring near the house, and beds were made from dry leaves for the two sisters. Everyone was tired, and

deer (*plural* **deer**) a small fast animal that lives in the forest and eats plants

spring a place where water comes up from the ground

only the two Mohicans stayed awake to **guard** the house from attack.

Later they woke up to hear men walking towards their hiding place. The Mohicans brought the horses into the house, and they waited to see what was going to happen.

Looking out of a dark window, Heyward saw about twenty Hurons coming through the trees. Suddenly they pointed to the stones where the dead Mohicans lay, and turned around and walked away again.

'They fear the ghosts of the dead,' said Hawk-eye.

When they were sure the Hurons had gone, Hawk-eye led the others out of the house towards Fort William Henry.

Later, from the top of a hill, they looked down into a valley. There, by moonlight, they could see Fort William Henry. Around it lay Montcalm's army.

'I hope we are not too late,' said Heyward worriedly.

A thick **fog** came down, but they travelled on. After some time Hawk-eye told Cora and Alice to get down from their horses and leave them in the forest.

'It's safer to walk now,' he explained.

Then they suddenly heard someone marching towards them.

'*Qui va là?*' asked a voice in French. 'Who goes there?'

'*Un ami de la France,*' answered Heyward. 'A friend of France.'

But the French soldier began shooting, and other Frenchmen joined him. Hawk-eye, Heyward, Cora, Alice, Gamut, and the Mohicans ran away from the bullets and disappeared into the fog. At last, a tall wooden building appeared in front of them.

'Shoot when they get close,' came a voice from the top of the wall.

'Father! Father! Don't shoot. It's Cora and me,' called Alice.

'Don't shoot, men!' cried General Munro. 'Open the door for my daughters. With them here, I will fight on even more bravely than before!'

guard to look after a place and stop people attacking it

fog low, thick cloud that makes it difficult to see

READING CHECK

Correct the underlined mistakes in the chapter summary.

Hawk-eye, Uncas, and Chingachgook appear slowly from behind some bushes. Magua and three other Hurons fight against Hawk-eye, the Munro sisters, and Heyward. Hawk-eye uses his gun to shoot the Huron who is wrestling with Heyward on the head. Then Heyward, Hawk-eye, and Uncas kill the Huron who is attacking Alice. Chingachgook thinks he has killed Uncas in the fight but then the 'dead' man runs away down the hill. After the fight, Uncas finds some wood and cooks some meat. The Mohicans, Hawk-eye, and the others eat, drink some water, and sing before they move on. They stay for the early part of the night in an old wooden house. About twenty Huron Indians surround the house at night, but they are afraid of wolves and so leave the place without attacking. When the Hurons leave, Hawk-eye and the others move on. In the thick fog they meet some English soldiers. In the end they reach Fort William Henry safely.

WORD WORK

Match the words in the house with the underlined words in the sentences.

a They eat some fast-moving animal meat before they travel on. ……deer……

b They can't see well because there is low cloud on the ground everywhere. ………………

c They drink water from the place where water comes from under the ground. ………………

d The Hurons are given a very unpleasant surprise when Hawk-eye kills one of them. ………………

e Magua and Chingachgook turn to one side and the other on the ground as they wrestle. ………………

f Magua runs off down the side of the hill. ………………

g The moment of winning is a great feeling. ………………

h The Mohicans watch and stop people from attacking the house in the forest all night. ………………

GUESS WHAT

What happens in the next chapter? Tick the boxes.

a Hawk-eye and the Mohicans . . .

1 ☐ leave Fort William Henry at once.

2 ☐ stay at Fort William Henry for some months.

3 ☐ say goodbye to each other at Fort William Henry.

b The French General, Montcalm . . .

1 ☐ kills everyone in Fort William Henry.

2 ☐ lets everyone in Fort William Henry leave.

3 ☐ kills the soldiers in Fort William Henry and lets the women and children leave.

c The Hurons attack . . .

1 ☐ the British soldiers from Fort William Henry.

2 ☐ the British women and children from Fort William Henry.

3 ☐ the French soldiers outside Fort William Henry.

CHAPTER 5

THE SIEGE OF FORT WILLIAM HENRY

General Munro welcomed Cora, Alice, and Heyward to Fort William Henry. Hawk-eye and the Mohicans left at once on other business

The fort was **surrounded** by the French and the Hurons. They attacked day and night with big guns, and still there was no word of the reinforcements promised by Webb. But under Munro's command, and with Heyward as second in command, the British soldiers were unafraid.

The French **siege** of William Henry went on for five days. On the fifth day, both commanders called a **truce**, and the fighting stopped for a while. During this time, Heyward took a walk along the high slope where the British guns stood outside the fort walls. He was surprised to see a French soldier walking along the path that led from Montcalm's **camp** to the fort. The man had a prisoner with him, and Heyward saw that it was Hawk-eye. His face was grim, his wrists were tied behind his back, and he had no rifle. Heyward turned and made his way to Munro's rooms at Fort William Henry. He thought that the French had caught Hawk-eye returning to the fort, and wondered why he had returned so soon. Perhaps Munro would know.

On his way he met Cora and Alice, who made fun of him for not spending much time with them.

'I am sorry,' he smiled, 'I do your father's business, as a soldier should. You cannot think badly of me for that?'

'Of course not, Duncan,' said Alice. 'In fact my sister and I are very grateful to you for bringing us here. Aren't we, Cora?'

'Ah!' replied Cora sadly. 'But what will happen now? These

surround to be all around something

siege when an army surrounds a building and waits for the people inside to stop fighting

truce when both armies agree to stop fighting for a short time

camp a place where you live in tents

are hard times for our father. How will this siege end?'

'In victory for the British, I hope,' replied Heyward, and he kissed Alice's hand, and then hurried on to Munro's room.

'Heyward,' said Munro opening his door. 'I wanted to talk to you.'

'About the message from the French, sir?'

'Yes. But let the Frenchmen wait a little. Is it true that you are in love with one of my daughters?'

'Yes,' answered Heyward. 'But I haven't told Alice yet.'

'Alice, you say! Do you have something against my Cora? Is it her dark skin? I met Cora's mother – my first wife – while I was fighting for the King in far off lands. Her great-grandparents came from Africa. Do you find that so ugly?'

'No, sir,' replied Heyward. 'It is only that Alice's smiling eyes and her happy laugh captured my heart first.'

'When Cora's mother died I returned to Scotland. Alice is the fair daughter of my second wife, who died when she was born,' went on Munro to himself, his face full of sadness.

Then he became calm and businesslike.

'Now let us talk of the scout Hawk-eye. He was returning from Fort Edward, but the French have taken him prisoner.'

'And are Webb's reinforcements coming?' asked Heyward.

'I have no word from Hawk-eye of that,' answered Munro. 'But he was bringing a letter from Webb which I'm sure explained everything. Montcalm has it now, of course. But if it brings bad news for us, why does Montcalm not tell us? Is that why he asks me to go and talk with him?'

'What will you do, sir? The fort walls cannot stand much longer against the siege, and many of our guns are useless.'

'I won't leave this fort while there is hope of help from Webb. Let us meet Montcalm and find out what we can.'

Some time later Munro and Heyward marched out of the fort at the head of their men to meet the French commander. Both sides stopped and stared for several minutes. Magua was there among Montcalm's men.

'So you come to talk of **peace**,' began Montcalm. 'My scouts tell me that you cannot hold the fort much longer. The time to be brave has passed. Think of the safety of your men now.'

'Have your scouts not also seen General Webb's reinforcements, which are on their way to us?'

'Let General Webb himself explain things,' replied Montcalm, and he brought out an open letter from his pocket and put it into Munro's hand.

Munro read it and his face went grey.

Sir,
It is impossible for me to send even one man to you. The best thing for you to do is to leave Fort William Henry as quickly as possible.
Yours,
Webb

'It's Webb's writing,' said Heyward reading it. 'It must be the captured letter.'

'We won't leave. We'll fight to the death,' said Munro.

'Wait,' interrupted Montcalm. 'The King of France is fair. You are brave, but there is no need to die. You can leave the fort with your men, women and children, your flags and guns, and my army will let you go.'

peace a time when there is no war

'I accept what you offer,' said Munro, and he turned to Heyward. 'It is strange to find an English **coward** and an honest Frenchman in one day.'

coward an easily frightened person

massacre the killing of a large number of people

hymn a song that people usually sing in a church

faint to suddenly feel weak and fall down

The next day, three thousand British left Fort William Henry, with Munro at the head of the line, a broken man. Heyward asked David Gamut, the singing teacher, to ride with Cora and Alice at the back of the line, with the other British women and children from the fort. On one side of them stood the French army; on the other, the Hurons watched and waited. When the British army had crossed the open ground in front of the fort and entered the forest the Hurons came near the women and children. Magua was with them.

Suddenly one of the Hurons took hold of a baby and pulled it from its mother's arms. She screamed and tried to get her child back, but he threw the baby to the ground and pulled out his tomahawk to attack and kill the mother.

This was how it began, the terrible **massacre** of the British women and children by the Hurons that day – and the French did nothing to stop it. David Gamut bravely sang **hymns** to stop the Indians attacking him and the Munro sisters, but suddenly Magua appeared before them.

'Come and be my wife!' he called to Cora, and Alice **fainted**.

'Never!' cried Cora.

Clever Magua then picked up Alice's body and ran with her towards the forest. Cora followed. Gamut came after her, still singing his hymns. The Hurons thought he was crazy and let him walk past freely.

At the forest's edge Magua took the sisters to two horses. He pushed Alice over the back of one, and Cora got up with her. He led the horse into the forest. Gamut, who wasn't far behind, got on the second horse, and rode after them.

READING CHECK

Match the sentences with the people.

Cora and Alice

Gamut

Hawk-eye

Heyward and Munro

Magua

Montcalm

a . . . leaves the fort at once with Uncas and Chingachgook.

b . . . comes back to the fort five days later as a prisoner of the French.

c . . . laugh at Heyward for being so busy that he has no time to be with them.

d . . . talk about Cora and Alice.

e . . . offers Munro the chance to leave Fort William Henry with his army and all the women and children of the fort.

f . . . go to talk with Montcalm.

g . . . is in the group of Indians with Montcalm.

h . . . does nothing to stop the massacre of Fort William Henry.

i . . . sings when the Hurons attack, and the Indians think he is mad.

j . . . takes Alice into the forest, and Cora and Gamut follow him.

WORD WORK

Find words from Chapter 5 to complete the sentences.

a The French army surrounds Fort William Henry on every side.

b The s_ _ _ _ of the fort goes on for many days and no British soldiers can go in or out during that time.

c At the end of that time the French and the English agree on a t_ _ _ _ and they stop fighting.

d Heyward goes with Munro to Montcalm's c_ _ _ where the French army are living.

e Montcalm says he doesn't want more fighting; he says he wants p_ _ _ _ .

f Gamut isn't a c_ _ _ _ _ ; he is very brave.

g When the Hurons attack the women and children of the fort, there is a m_ _ _ _ _ _ _ and lots of helpless people die.

h When Magua asks Cora to be his wife, Alice f_ _ _ _ _ and falls down onto the ground.

i Gamut likes to sing h_ _ _ _ .

GUESS WHAT

What happens in the next chapter?
Tick the boxes.

		Yes	Perhaps	No
a	Magua kills Alice and makes Cora his wife.	☐	☐	☐
b	Heyward, Munro, Hawk-eye, and the Mohicans go to look for Cora and Alice.	☐	☐	☐
c	Chingachgook and Uncas find Magua's tracks.	☐	☐	☐
d	Montcalm moves into Fort William Henry.	☐	☐	☐
e	Munro goes to Fort Edward to get help.	☐	☐	☐
f	Hawk-eye wants to travel by canoe across the lake.	☐	☐	☐
g	The Hurons attack Hawk-eye, Heyward, Munro, and the Mohicans.	☐	☐	☐

CHAPTER 6

TRACKS FROM THE BATTLEFIELD

Three days after the terrible massacre at Fort William Henry, about an hour before the sun went down, five figures crossed the empty battleground, now silent and still. The two in front, Uncas and Chingachgook, looked all around them as they moved forwards. They were followed by Hawk-eye, Heyward and Munro. These last two had taken off their British army uniforms and heavy boots. They were now dressed in the soft **leather** jackets and trousers, and the light **moccasins**, of scouts. It was a dangerous business which they had in front of them, following the French army as it marched north.

Fort William Henry was now nothing but a black smoking **ruin**. The French had not wished to capture and keep it, only to destroy it after taking it. They hoped in this way to stop the British from using the fort in the future as a useful place from which to push northwards into Canada.

Slowly the five figures moved across the grim battlefield looking at the many lifeless bodies of women and children that still lay where they had fallen. They were searching for Cora and Alice, but they did not find them amongst the dead.

Then, Uncas found something caught on the branch of a tree. It was a small piece of green scarf, just like the one Cora usually wore. Heyward and Munro went over to look.

'Many thanks, my friends!' cried Munro. 'My daughters left the battle alive, then, but where have they gone since?'

Chingachgook followed some tracks which led into the forest, and the others came after him. Suddenly he pointed down at something. There was a moccasin shape in the soft ground.

Heyward came nearer and looked where Chingachgook was

leather made of animal skin

moccasin an Indian shoe made of soft leather

ruin an old building that is falling down

pointing. 'So, they were prisoners,' he said.

Uncas now got on his hands and knees and looked closely at the shape in the soft ground. Indians can read moccasin tracks better than white men.

'Well, boy?' asked Hawk-eye. 'Whose is it?'

Uncas looked up. 'Magua!' he said, and Chingachgook agreed.

'So Magua took Cora this way,' added Hawk-eye.

'But not Alice?' asked Heyward.

Then they found Gamut's hymn book on the ground.

'So that good man went with them, too,' said Heyward.

A little way into the forest they saw the tracks of the horses, and at last they found something to tell them that Alice, too, had passed that way – one of her **ear-rings**. Heyward picked it up quietly and put it in his pocket, and Munro cried, thinking of his two poor daughters in Magua's hands.

Because Munro was so weak with worry, the five stayed that evening in the ruins of the fort. After a light supper of dry **bear** meat, Munro went to sleep immediately, but Heyward and the others stayed awake to guard the place. In the middle of the night they heard something moving amongst the dead bodies on the battlefield.

'Wolves, perhaps, looking for food,' said Heyward.

'I'm not so sure of that,' said Hawk-eye, and he called Uncas to him. The two men talked **briefly** together, and then Uncas took a rifle and **crawled** off.

Chingachgook sat calmly by the fire. You couldn't tell that he believed that there were Hurons out on the battlefield.

Suddenly there was a rifle shot, and the old Mohican threw himself to the ground. The bullet missed him by inches and hit the wall of the fort just behind him. Then there was another shot out on the battlefield. Soon after that Uncas returned.

'Hurons?' asked Hawk-eye.

'One,' replied Uncas, lifting up one finger as he spoke.

Chingachgook, Uncas, and Hawk-eye now sat in a circle

ear-ring a ring that you wear in your ear

bear a large four-legged animal

briefly for a short time

crawl to move on the ground on your hands and knees

persuade to make somebody change their way of thinking

paddle to move a canoe through the water with a long flat piece of wood

near the fire. They lit a pipe and smoked as they spoke of what to do the next day. Heyward watched them with interest.

At first Uncas and Chingachgook wanted to follow Magua and his prisoners on foot, but after a lot of talking and smoking, Hawk-eye **persuaded** them to travel by canoe across the lake. After an hour, they finished their conversation, and lay down to sleep. Heyward was not long in following their example.

The stars were still in the sky when Hawk-eye woke them early the next morning. Heyward and Munro followed him down to the lake and got into the canoe. Uncas and Chingachgook were already there, ready to **paddle** away. Hawk-eye got in last, and they left, steering across the beautiful waters of the lake.

As the sun came up they found themselves at the narrow part of the lake, with lots of small islands in their path. This was the path that Montcalm had taken to return to the North. Perhaps he had left some of his men behind to guard his back, so Uncas and Chingachgook paddled forwards slowly, careful of possible danger. As they got near to one small island, Chingachgook pointed. There was grey smoke above the trees.

'Someone's lit a fire!' said Hawk-eye. 'But there can't be many of them.'

'Then let us attack!' said Heyward. But he spoke a little too loudly, and suddenly there came a rifle shot from the island,

and two canoes pushed into the water, each full of Huron fighters. Chingachgook and Uncas paddled off, faster than the wind, between two other rocky islands. Then Hawk-eye gave his paddle to Heyward and picked up his rifle from the bottom of the canoe.

'Start paddling, Heyward,' he shouted, 'while I see if my rifle "Kill-deer" can reach them.'

As their canoe flew across the lake, Hawk-eye lifted his rifle to his eye to shoot at the leader of the Hurons in the canoe that was following them; but a cry from Uncas stopped him. Looking forward, the scout at once saw why he had cried out. A third Huron canoe had come from one of the islands in front of them, and was cutting across their path.

Uncas and Chingachgook steered the boat quickly around a long low island, and the canoe in front had to slow down in order to steer along the other side of the island. Hawk-eye lifted his rifle again, and shot at the Huron in the front of the canoe, who fell back dying. As the Hurons did not have rifles that could reach as far as 'Kill-deer', and as none of them could paddle as fast as the two Mohicans, they gave up their chase.

Some time later Hawk-eye, the Mohicans, Heyward, and Munro landed at the edge of the lake, hid their canoe carefully under some bushes, picked up their bags and their guns, and walked off into the forest.

READING CHECK

Tick the boxes to complete the sentences.

a Heyward, Munro, and the others are looking for . . .

1 ☐ Montcalm

2 ☑ Cora and Alice

b Uncas finds a piece of a green scarf that belongs to . . .

1 ☐ Cora

2 ☐ Alice

c Chingachgook finds tracks made by . . . on the ground.

1 ☐ Montcalm

2 ☐ Magua

d . . . feels weak with worry about Cora and Alice.

1 ☐ Heyward

2 ☐ Munro

e That night a Huron Indian shoots at . . .

1 ☐ Uncas

2 ☐ Chingachgook

f . . . persuades the Mohicans to go after Magua in a canoe.

1 ☐ Heyward

2 ☐ Hawk-eye

g . . . shoots at some Hurons, and he and the others escape from the Huron canoes.

1 ☐ Hawk-eye

2 ☐ Uncas

WORD WORK

Find words from Chapter 6 to complete the sentences.

a They have moccasins on their feet.

b They are also wearing _ _ _ _ _ _ _ _ jackets and trousers.

c The fort is a _ _ _ _ after the French destroy it.

d They find Alice's _ _ _ – _ _ _ _ on the ground.

e They rest at the fort and have some dry _ _ _ _ meat to eat.

f Uncas and Hawk-eye talk _ _ _ _ _ _ _ _ because they have very little time.

g Uncas _ _ _ _ _ _ _ off on his hands and knees to see what is making a noise at night.

h The Mohicans want to go after Magua on land, but Hawk-eye _ _ _ _ _ _ _ _ _ _ them to go across the lake.

i The Mohicans _ _ _ _ _ _ to make their canoe move across the lake.

GUESS WHAT

What do Hawk-eye, Heyward, Munro, and the Mohicans do in the next chapter? Tick one box.

a ☐ They kill Magua.

b ☐ They find Gamut.

c ☐ They rescue Alice.

d ☐ They rescue Cora.

e ☐ They fight the Hurons.

An Ojibwa hunter

CHAPTER 7

INTO THE HURON CAMP

Once they had left their canoe, Hawk-eye, the two Mohicans, Heyward, and Munro travelled on over land. They were crossing that wild country – of valleys and mountains – that stands between Lake Champlain and the springs where the Hudson, Mohawk, and Saint Lawrence rivers begin.

After their day's journey they lit a fire, ate, and then slept. They woke early next morning and continued northwards. Hawk-eye looked around for the tracks of Magua and his prisoners, but without success.

'Well,' he said, 'I'm sure they came this way, but where?'

Uncas pointed to some tracks a little higher up the hill. 'Horses went this way,' he said. 'Dark-hair goes north.'

They followed the **prints** left by the horses until they found a place where Magua had stopped. Black pieces of wood lay on the ground, all that was left of a fire, and there were tracks all around. Not far away they found the two riderless horses eating grass. They were dirty and had clearly been left to go free a day or two before.

'Not far to go,' said Hawk-eye. 'We must be in enemy country.'

Uncas found another track, made by a big man in moccasins.

'Gamut,' said Hawk-eye, after looking at the prints.

'But where are the others' tracks?' asked Heyward.

'I'm sure Magua made the young ladies put their feet where the singer had stepped,' said Hawk-eye. 'An old Indian **trick**.'

He was right. Later the Munro sisters' prints appeared next to Gamut's tracks.

'My poor girls,' said General Munro, looking sadly down at the small prints. 'Will they survive in this wild place?'

'Oh yes, they are strong enough. But looking at the singing

prints tracks made by feet on the ground

trick a clever way of doing something

teacher's tracks, I can see that he is tired and weak now.'

They followed the tracks until they came to a lake. Then they decided to explore in groups. Uncas and Chingachgook went one way, Hawk-eye and Munro a second way, and Heyward a third. The light was going, and it was difficult to see, but to Heyward's eyes there seemed to be a group of low round buildings at the water's edge, and dark shapes, like Indians on their hands and knees, were moving between them.

Heyward was going to give a bird call, to warn the others, when he suddenly saw the figure of an Indian in the darkness nearby. Heyward stood watching and waiting. The Indian had four **feathers** in his hair, and thick **paint** covered his face. He wore moccasins on his feet, had a shirt tied around his middle, and a **cloak** over his shoulders.

Suddenly Hawk-eye appeared at Heyward's side. Heyward pointed to the unknown Indian and whispered to the scout.

feather this comes from the tail of a bird

paint colour that you put on with a brush

cloak a coat with no arms

'Look over there. We can't move freely with him watching.'

Hawk-eye studied the tall figure.

'He isn't a Huron,' he said, 'that's for sure. In fact I don't recognize which of the Canadian tribes he comes from.'

'Well, he isn't carrying a rifle or a knife, so if he doesn't call to his Indian friends in the village by the lake he isn't a danger.'

'His Indian friends!' said Hawk-eye, laughing to himself. 'Well, well. I think I'll go and get a closer look at him. Keep your rifle ready. But don't shoot until I say.'

Hawk-eye moved closer and closer to the strange figure and soon stood behind him. Hawk-eye lifted his hands, ready to catch the man by the shoulders, when suddenly there came a loud noise of something hitting the water. The dark shapes disappeared into the lake and swam off.

Hawk-eye dropped his hands and laughed. 'What mistakes a man can make!' he laughed. 'You're no Indian,' he said to the figure, 'but our old friend Mr Gamut! And that Indian village by the lake,' he said, turning to Heyward, 'is no home for Indians, but a place built by **beavers**.'

Then Hawk-eye gave a bird call, and the Mohicans and Munro came back from the lake towards them.

'We found the singing teacher waiting to teach the beavers a hymn or two, and dressed as a Huron,' Hawk-eye explained once they had arrived.

'And Cora and Alice?' asked Heyward quickly.

'They are prisoners of the Indians,' replied Gamut. 'But they are well and they are unhurt.'

'Thank goodness!' cried Munro. 'Oh, my poor dear daughters.'

Gamut then told them of his journey. Magua had not chased him away, because, like most Indians, he would not touch anyone who was crazy, believing that they were specially cared for by the **Great Spirit**.

'And where is Magua now?' asked Hawk-eye.

beaver a brown animal with big front teeth and a flat tail that lives in lakes

Great Spirit the Indians' god

'He is **hunting** today with his men. They are looking for **moose**, and tomorrow they will go north through the forest, towards Canada.'

'And my daughters?' asked Munro.

'Cora is with a tribe who live beyond that mountain over there, and Alice is with the Huron women not far from here.'

'But why are you not guarded?' asked Hawk-eye.

'I am only a singer. They do not worry where I go.'

'But why did you not escape and go back to Fort Edward?'

'And leave the sisters with the Indians?' asked Gamut.

'So Cora is with a tribe just past that mountain,' said Heyward.

'Yes,' said Gamut. 'I don't remember their name, but they are friends of the French.'

'Tell us about them,' said Hawk-eye, and Uncas and Chingachgook listened carefully. 'Did you see the **totems** of the tribe?'

'Well,' said Gamut. 'They had strange pictures painted on them. One was a terrible, huge **tortoise**.'

'Delawares!' said Chingachgook.

'Interesting,' added Hawk-eye. 'Delawares and Mohicans come from the same great Indian family. Chingachgook is a great chief of the tortoises. If Cora is with the Delawares that could be very useful.'

'What are we waiting for? Let's save Cora and Alice at once,' said Heyward.

'Well,' said Hawk-eye. 'I think we should let the singing teacher go and tell the sisters about us. He can go here and there without any problem.'

'Paint me so that no one will recognize me,' said Heyward. 'I'll pretend to be a crazy French actor from a travelling theatre group. You go to the Delawares and save Cora, and I'll go with Gamut to save Alice.'

So they painted Heyward's face, and soon he was ready. Before he left with Gamut, Hawk-eye talked to him. 'Munro's

hunt to look for and kill animals

moose (*plural* **moose**) a large animal like a deer with big horns on its head

totem an animal that is special to an Indian tribe

tortoise a slow-moving animal with a hard shell on its body

weak and **confused**. I'll leave him here with Chingachgook, while Uncas and I go to the Delawares.'

So Heyward and Gamut walked off, past the beaver lake. After some time they reached the Huron camp, where they saw a group of boys playing in the long grass. The children stopped their games and hid in the grass when they saw their visitors getting closer. Their cries brought several adult Indians to the door of the nearest long wooden **hut**.

Gamut of course was known to the Hurons and used to their ways. He walked to the long hut and entered it. Heyward followed. They both sat on the floor of the hut, which was dark except for the light of a burning **torch**. Three Huron chiefs sat opposite, and several Hurons stood near them, listening and watching, waiting for their visitors to speak.

At last one of the old chiefs spoke to them in Huron.

'Does anyone speak French?' answered Heyward, in that language.

'What does Montcalm, our Canadian father, say to the Hurons who killed the English five days ago?' asked one of the old chiefs, in French.

'I imagine he is pleased and says the Hurons are brave.'

'No. He turns his back on us and looks behind him.'

'He looks to see no enemies are following, perhaps.'

'The English are dead,' went on the chief, 'but he opens his ears to the Delawares. They tell him lies about us.'

'This cannot be,' said Heyward, changing his plan. 'He sends me, a medicine man, to help any Hurons who are ill.'

'A medicine man? Then why is your face covered in paint? Your kind of medicine men have white faces.'

'When an Indian chief goes to speak to his white fathers, he wears the shirt that they offer him. My brother gave me paint, and I wear it.'

They seemed pleased with this reply, but suddenly the calm was broken by some Huron fighters noisily returning to the

confused not thinking clearly

hut a small wooden house

torch a stick burning at one end that people use to see in the dark

village after a fight with a neighbouring tribe. With the other Indians, Heyward left the hut to see what was happening. A group of Huron men stood there with two prisoners. One was a Huron, and the other was Uncas, the Mohican.

Suddenly Uncas broke free and bravely tried to escape. Heyward put out his foot, and the Huron who was running closely behind Uncas **tripped** over it, but in the end they caught the Mohican and brought him, together with the Huron prisoner, into the long hut.

trip to fall because something is in front of your feet

wise intelligent, clever

reed a tall thin straight plant that grows in or near water

'Delaware,' said the Huron chief to Uncas. 'Two of our men are chasing the white scout, your friend. When they catch him, we will take you both to our **wise** men who will say if you must live or die.'

'I heard two shots from my friend's rifle,' replied Uncas. 'Perhaps your men will not come back.'

'If the Delawares are so clever, why are you here as prisoner?'

'I ran after this man,' said Uncas, pointing at the Huron prisoner, 'and like a coward he ran from me. I was caught by a trick.'

An old woman now came close holding a wooden torch. She looked at Uncas. He looked back at her unafraid. She then looked at the Huron, who shook in front of her.

'Shaking-**reed**,' said the old woman. 'You are good-looking. But in battle you are a coward, and you must die.'

She drove a knife into the shaking Huron's heart, throwing her torch to the ground. Darkness filled the hut.

READING CHECK

What do they say? Complete the sentences.

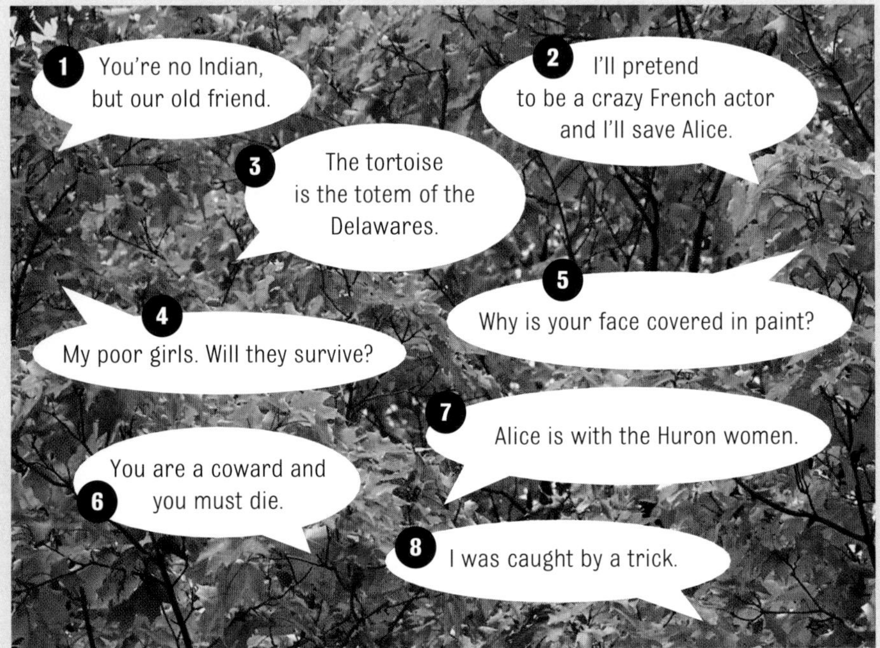

a After looking at his daughters' prints on the ground, Munro says, 'My poor girls. Will they survive?'

b Hawk-eye says to Gamut ....

c .... Gamut tells them.

d .... says Chingachgook.

e Heyward says, ...

f .... asks an old Huron chief.

g .... says Uncas in the Huron camp.

h An old Huron woman tells Shaking-reed, ...

WORD WORK

Use the words below in their correct form to complete Heyward's diary.

print
trick
feather
paint
beaver
hunt
moose
totem
tortoise
confused
hut
wise
torch

We followed Magua's **(a)** ..prints.......... *and arrived at a lake with lots of* **(b)** .... *swimming in it. A strange man with brightly-coloured* **(c)** .... *on his face and four* **(d)** .... *in his hair was watching them. At first we were* **(e)** .... *and thought that he was an Indian, but then we saw that it was Gamut. Gamut told us that Magua was busy* **(f)** .... *with his men, looking for* **(g)** .... *to kill. I painted my face, hoping to get into the Huron camp by using a* **(h)** .... *– saying I was a doctor. Hawk-eye and Uncas went to the Delaware camp. Chingachgook says that the Delawares'* **(i)** .... *animal is the* **(j)** ...., *and that the Delawares are friends of the Mohicans. When I got to the Huron camp I went into the meeting* **(k)** .... *where the* **(l)** .... *men and chiefs were sitting. An old woman holding a* **(m)** .... *came in to speak to a cowardly Huron Indian.*

GUESS WHAT

What happens in the next chapter? Tick the boxes.	**Yes**	**No**
a Munro arrives at the Huron camp.	☐	☐
b Magua arrives at the Huron camp.	☐	☐
c Magua says Uncas must die the next day.	☐	☐
d Magua kills Uncas.	☐	☐
e Heyward finds Alice.	☐	☐
f Alice agrees to marry Heyward.	☐	☐
g Heyward, Hawk-eye, and Alice escape from the Hurons.	☐	☐
h Cora escapes alone from the Delaware village.	☐	☐

CHAPTER 8

A BEAR TO THE RESCUE

When the torch hit the floor and went out, all the Indians in the hut – it seemed – ran outside. Heyward thought he was alone in the hut with the dead Huron. But just then Uncas came close and spoke to him.

'Go,' he said, and pushed him to the door of the hut.

Heyward went out. He looked into some of the nearby huts to see if he could find Alice, but without success. Then he turned to look for the singing teacher. But Gamut was nowhere to be seen, so Heyward returned to the long hut with the other Indians. A torch burnt in the place again, and Heyward sat down. Uncas stood in the middle of the hut as before.

Then one of the older Hurons spoke to Heyward. 'An **evil** spirit lives in the wife of one of my young men. Can you frighten it away?'

'I will try,' replied Heyward.

Just then a Huron **warrior** entered and sat down next to Heyward. It was Magua. The Hurons now lit a pipe, which they passed between them.

'Welcome, Magua!' said an old chief. 'How was the hunting?'

'We killed many moose. My men are bringing them to the village now. If Shaking-reed walks along the hunting path he will meet them.'

They all fell silent when they heard the dead Huron's name.

Shaking-reed's father spoke. 'Shaking-reed was a coward, his blood was **pale**, and he is forgotten. He was no Huron. The Great Spirit has decided that my family should end with me.' Grimly the old man left the hut.

'Delawares have been here,' said another of the chiefs to Magua. 'But we Hurons do not sleep.'

evil very bad

warrior a fighter

pale without colour

'Delawares?' cried Magua angrily. 'Did you kill them?'

'No, but one of them is our prisoner,' said the old chief, pointing at the young warrior who still stood, without moving, in the middle of the hut.

Magua got up and went over to look at the prisoner. The Mohican stared back at him, a grim look on his face. Magua's face filled with a look of evil victory.

'Uncas!' he cried. All the Indians in the hut cried out when they heard the name of their most hated enemy. The prisoner smiled to see that he was so well-known.

'Mohican, you die!' said Magua in English. Then he told the other Hurons about the fight at Glenn's Waterfall, and the death of so many fine Huron warriors. He told them about Hawk-eye's attack and how that had ended.

'We killed many English,' he finished. 'But the only way to pay for our Huron dead is with Indian blood. So we should kill this Mohican.'

All the Hurons in the hut were hungry for blood by now, and one tried to attack Uncas there and then with his tomahawk, but Magua stopped him. Heyward watched all this, helpless, not knowing what to do.

'Be patient, my brothers,' said Magua. 'We mustn't kill him quickly tonight. No, let him die tomorrow under the strong light of the sun, with all our women there to see his body shake like the coward that he is.'

Several Hurons came forward, tied Uncas's arms behind his back and marched him from the long hut into a smaller prison hut next door. Once they had thrown the Mohican inside, five of them stood outside to guard the place.

Now the chief who had asked for Heyward's help with the sick woman stood up and asked the white medicine man to go with him. Heyward followed him into the night. They crossed the village and went towards a nearby hill. Suddenly in their path they saw the dark figure of a bear. The Huron chief walked past the animal without fear. Heyward decided that it was probably a bear which belonged to the tribe. As they passed it, the bear began to follow Heyward, and he felt uncomfortable, especially as it began to **growl**. Finally they reached the hillside, where the old chief opened a wooden door and they entered a cave. Still the bear followed.

The cave that they went into was under the hill, and there were a number of smaller rooms joined by passages. The chief led Heyward into one of these rooms, where the sick woman lay on a bed, with several Huron women around her. In the middle of these women was Gamut, the singing teacher. He began to sing a beautiful hymn, and at once the bear joined him, growling with the music.

Suddenly Gamut stopped, and said to Heyward: 'The woman you are searching for is near.' Then he left the cave.

Heyward went to the Huron woman lying on her bed. One look was enough to tell him that she was very ill indeed. Again the bear growled, and every time Heyward moved towards her he growled again.

'Our bear wants us to leave. Some things must stay secret,' said the old chief. 'Come, you women. Let us leave this white man to make a strong medicine that will help our sister, who is so ill.'

The chief led the women from the cave and Heyward found himself alone with the sick woman and the bear. The animal came close to Heyward, lifted its **paws** up to its head, and pulled it off. Heyward's mouth fell open. Then under the bear's head, he was pleased to see the well-known face of his old friend Hawk-eye.

'Don't make a noise,' said the scout. 'There are Hurons near.'

'But how did you get here?' asked Heyward in a low voice.

'Well, I left Chingachgook and old Munro hidden safely in one of the empty beavers' houses, and then Uncas and I went

growl to make a deep, angry noise

paw an animal's foot

off to the village of the Delawares. On the way we met a group of Hurons and fought them. Uncas ran off after one of them and that was the last I saw of him.'

'He was brought here as a prisoner,' said Heyward. 'I saw him arrive, but could do nothing to help him.'

'I thought that he was a prisoner,' said Hawk-eye. 'That's why I came here.'

'But what about your bear suit?'

'Well, after shooting the rest of the Hurons, I came to this village and passed the hut where the medicine man lives. I hit him over the head, tied him up, **gagged** him and got into his bear suit. But where's Alice?'

'I don't know. I couldn't find her.'

'Don't you remember what Gamut said: "The woman you are looking for is near." Didn't you understand? I believe he meant that Alice is here, in one of the rooms in this cave.'

'Then I must go to her at once!' cried Heyward.

'Wait,' said Hawk-eye. 'Take off that face paint first. You don't want to frighten the girl. We can paint you again later.'

Heyward cleaned the paint off his face and went to look for Alice. He soon found her in a nearby room. 'There's no time now, to tell you everything,' he said. 'But we must leave this cave and find your father. He's weak and confused now, but before he became ill, I told him about my feelings for you, and he agreed to you marrying me. What do you say?'

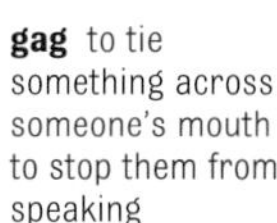

gag to tie something across someone's mouth to stop them from speaking

'Oh Duncan,' replied Alice quietly. 'This is not a time to talk of things like that. Take me to my father first.'

Heyward was going to reply when he was interrupted by a hand on his shoulder. He turned to find the evil Magua standing in front of him. He had come into the cave by a different door, and he now closed it and put sticks and stones in front of it so that it could not easily be opened again.

'**Palefaces** catch beavers, but Hurons catch English,' he laughed.

Seeing Magua so close, Alice fainted and fell to the floor.

Then the bear, with its head in place, appeared and began to growl. Magua thought it was the medicine man and said: '**Fool**, go to the women and children. This is men's work.'

The bear stood up, its paws in the air, and came towards Magua. Suddenly, it put its arms round him and held him close. Heyward immediately tied his wrists and ankles with rope and gagged him. After that Heyward and Hawk-eye carried Alice to the room where the sick woman lay. They took the blanket from her bed and put it over Alice. Then Heyward picked her up, and Hawk-eye explained his plan.

'Tell the Hurons that the evil spirit has gone from the sick woman, but that you want to take her into the forest to give her some different medicines.'

They went outside to the chief and the Huron women.

'How is my wife?' asked the woman's worried husband.

'The spirit has left her and is a prisoner in the rocks, so you mustn't enter the cave,' said Heyward. 'We are now going to the forest for medicine and will return later.'

So, Hawk-eye, Heyward and Alice reached the forest. At its edge Hawk-eye told the others the way to the Delaware village.

'Now I must **rescue** Uncas,' he said, and he returned to the Huron village.

Once there, he went to a little old hut where he heard Gamut singing. He went straight in, and Gamut stared at him.

paleface an Indian name for a white person

fool a stupid person

rescue to save from danger

'Don't you know me?' asked Hawk-eye, who was still in the bear suit. 'It's me, Hawk-eye. We must rescue Uncas. Take me to his hut.'

Gamut led Hawk-eye to the prison hut, where one of the guards spoke English. He explained that the medicine man wanted to blow on the prisoner to make sure, by **magic**, that he was a shaking coward the next day. The guards let them pass, and moved away. They didn't want to be blown on. In the hut, Hawk-eye untied Uncas, and took off his bear suit.

'Put this on,' he said to the Mohican. 'Now Mr Singing Teacher, we must **exchange** clothes. You take my leather jacket and trousers, and I'll take your hat and your cloak.'

Uncas quickly got into the bear suit, while Gamut and Hawk-eye put on their new clothes. Then Hawk-eye spoke to Gamut.

'You must lie down and pretend to be Uncas. When they find you, the Hurons will be angry, but you'll be safe, because they think the Great Spirit **protects** you. Will you help us?'

'Of course,' said Gamut, and he lay on the floor.

Hawk-eye and Uncas left the hut with no problem. They were walking into the forest when suddenly they heard a cry from the Huron village. Uncas took off the bear suit and Hawk-eye pulled two rifles from under a bush.

'Now we're ready for them,' said the scout.

magic something that is mysterious and which you cannot explain

exchange to give something and to get something different back

protect to keep someone safe from danger

READING CHECK

Correct the mistakes in these sentences.

a An Indian chief asks Gamut to help the wife of one of his men.

b Magua has a look of evil victory on his face when he sees Heyward.

c A moose follows Heyward and the Huron chief.

d Heyward goes into a hut to help a sick Huron woman.

e Munro is hiding inside the animal skin.

f Heyward and Alice tie up Magua.

g Heyward and Hawk-eye take Cora into the forest in the sick woman's blanket.

h Hawk-eye takes Uncas's place in the prison hut.

WORD WORK

1 Find ten more words from Chapter 8 in the Indian blanket.

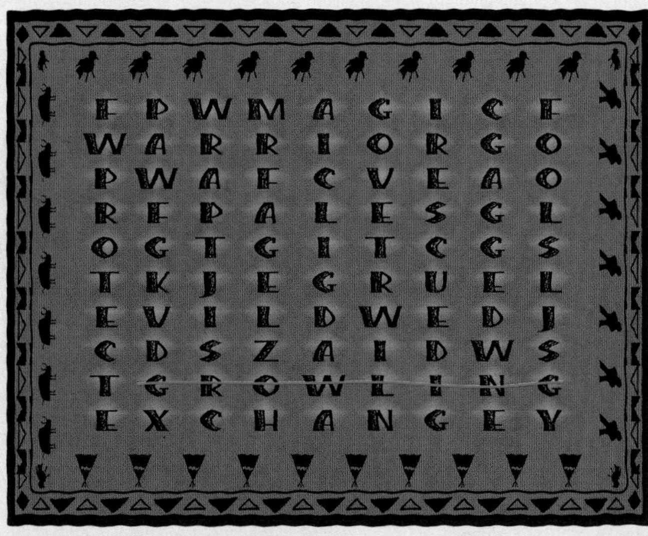

2 Complete the sentences with the words from Activity 1.

a 'That bear's .growling... .'
'Yes. I think it's got something painful in its ....'

b And then the young soldier .... her from the old chief, who wasn't good at all; he was ....

c 'This stone is .... It can help you.'
'Oh, good! Will it .... me from danger?'

d 'You aren't intelligent. You're a ....'
'And you aren't a brave .... You're a coward.'

e 'There's the girl! She can't speak because someone has .... her.'
'And there's no colour in her face because she's .... with fear.'

f 'Can I .... these pesos for dollars?'

GUESS WHAT

What happens in the next chapter? Tick the boxes.

a When the Hurons find out that Uncas has escaped, they . . .
- **1** ☐ attack the Delaware village.
- **2** ☐ go to look for Magua.
- **3** ☐ kill Gamut.

b Magua . . .
- **1** ☐ becomes a Huron chief.
- **2** ☐ is not found and dies in the cave.
- **3** ☐ makes friends with the Mohicans.

c Heyward and Alice . . .
- **1** ☐ get married.
- **2** ☐ go to the beavers' lake to find Munro.
- **3** ☐ reach the Delaware village safely.

d Hawk-eye and Uncas . . .
- **1** ☐ are taken prisoner by the French.
- **2** ☐ attack the Huron village.
- **3** ☐ become prisoners of the Delawares.

A chief of the Flathead tribe.

CHAPTER 9

MAGUA, HURON CHIEF

After some time the Huron guards who were standing near Uncas's prison hut decided that they were no longer afraid of the medicine man's magic. They came closer, and looked in through the door at their prisoner. At first Gamut had his back to them and his feet pulled up, and they believed he was Uncas, but then he straightened his legs and turned, and they saw his face. At once they realized the trick which the singer and the others had played on them, and they were very angry. But, when Gamut started singing – to stop himself from becoming frightened – they remembered that he was a fool. Instead of attacking him, they ran through the village and warned the others in their tribe of their prisoner's escape.

Soon two hundred Hurons were awake, and they began to run towards the long hut to discover what had happened. They looked around for Magua, but could find him nowhere.

Some of the fastest warriors went to make sure that their enemies, the Delaware, were not attacking the village. Women and children ran about here and there, and the whole place was full of noise and hurried steps.

At last the old chiefs arrived, took their places in the middle of the long **council** hut, and began to talk together in low voices. Then, suddenly, a group of Indians arrived with the village medicine man. He told them briefly how someone had hit him on the head and stolen his bear suit. Then the father of the sick woman told his story, and he and ten Hurons went off to the caves to see what they could find there.

When they entered the place, they found the sick woman still on her bed, although many thought that they had seen the white man carry her to the forest. Then the woman's

council the group of important people who talk about and decide what happens in a village

father looked at her and saw that she was dead.

'The Great Spirit is angry with us!' he cried.

One of the older Indians was going to reply when something long and dark rolled out of the next room in the cave into the middle of the room where they were standing. For a moment no one knew what it was, but when it sat up, and they could see its angry face, they realized that it was Magua. Several warriors stepped forwards and cut the ropes around his ankles and wrists, and the gag that stopped his mouth.

Magua stood up, and an angry light shone from his eyes. It was lucky for them that Hawk-eye and Heyward were nowhere near him at that moment.

Then an old chief spoke. 'You have an enemy. Tell us where he is, and we will kill him for you.'

'Let the Mohican die!'

There was a moment of silence and then the same old chief replied. 'He runs fast, but my young men run after him.'

'Has he escaped?' asked Magua in a shocked voice.

'An evil spirit came among us and closed our eyes to what was happening,' replied the old man.

'That was no evil spirit. It was "Long-rifle".'

Many Hurons cried out at once when they heard that name, so hateful to their ears.

'Let us go to the council hut,' said Magua.

He then led them to the long hut. When they were all in their places, they looked at Magua, and he began to speak. He told the story of what had happened to him in the cave. Hawk-eye's trick was now fully explained to the whole tribe.

The Indians in the council hut were now angry and ready to listen to more of Magua's evil words. He cleverly worked on them, persuading them that it was time to attack their enemies, and that they would have a great victory. They all agreed with him, and it was decided that Magua himself should be the chief who would lead them in this battle. This was a

prepare to get ready

cousin a close person in your family

great moment for Magua, for, by luck and cleverness, he had now managed to get back all that he had lost when he left his tribe all those years before to work for the British.

He at once sent spies to the Delaware village, and ordered his warriors to go to their huts, telling them to make themselves ready. Then he went to his own hut to **prepare** himself.

Before the sun came up the next day, twenty Indians came to Magua. They carried rifles, but for the moment the paint on their faces spoke of peace, not war. Magua led them out of the village, and past the lake. One of the Hurons had the beaver as his totem, so he stopped and spoke to these animals.

'**Cousins**,' he said in a friendly voice, 'We protect you from the hunters, and we will go on protecting you, so be grateful. Now help us. We are going to visit our old enemies the Delawares, to see if "Long-rifle" and the Mohican, Uncas, are hiding with them. Give us your cleverness and help our tongues to work well when we speak to the Delaware chief.'

In this way he spoke to his cousins the beavers, and he was happy to see their dark heads appear from time to time

above the water as they swam around in the lake. When he finished speaking, he also saw a large beaver head look out briefly at him from a large old ruined **lodge** which he had thought was empty. This seemed to him a very lucky **sign**.

The Hurons marched on towards the village of the Delawares. Nobody looked behind them, and nobody saw the big dark head again stare out from the door of the old beavers' lodge and watch them. It seemed strangely intelligent. Then, when the Hurons entered the forest, all was explained. Now Magua and the others were gone, a man in a beaver's **mask** crawled out of the ruined lodge. It was Chingachgook.

The Delawares were **allies** of the French, and, like the Hurons, they had followed Montcalm into British lands. But when the French had most needed their help, the Delawares had refused it. When Montcalm sent messages to them, the Delaware chiefs replied that their tomahawks could no longer cut well, and that they needed time to make them bright and **sharp** again. The French had decided that it was better to keep the Delawares as allies who were not helping them, and not make them into enemies who were fighting against them; so they left things as they were.

When the sun came up over the Delaware village, it shone down on a busy place. The women ran from hut to hut. Some were preparing the morning meal, others exchanged hurried whispered conversations with their sisters. The warriors sat around, talking. Rifles stood ready for the hunt, but no one went hunting, and here and there a man was cleaning his gun in a way which was strange when there were no enemies except wild animals. From time to time, one or another of the Delawares looked towards a large hut in the middle of the village. It seemed to contain something important for them.

Into this scene came a figure. He appeared on a high rock at the edge of the village, lifted his arm to the sky and then

lodge a house that a beaver makes for itself from wooden sticks

sign a thing that shows without words that something will happen

mask something that you wear to cover your face

ally a friend who fights on your side in a war

sharp good for cutting with

put his hand on his chest in a sign of peace. The Delawares saw the sign and welcomed him. He climbed down from the rock and walked into the middle of the huts with many signs of peace to the Delawares whom he met on the way. Silently he walked towards the Delaware chiefs. When he got close, they saw that he was Magua, the Huron chief.

'Welcome,' said Chief Hard-heart as he and Magua shook hands.

After this the Delaware invited the Huron to his hut, to eat breakfast with him, and Magua accepted the invitation. Once the short meal was finished, the two began talking again.

'Your tomahawks have been red with blood,' said Hard-heart.

'But now they are clean and no longer sharp,' replied Magua. 'The English are dead and the Delawares are our neighbours.'

Hard-heart lifted his hand in a sign of peace, but said nothing.

'Does my prisoner give you trouble?' continued the Huron.

'She is welcome,' replied the Delaware.

Magua said nothing for a while, and then he asked.

'Have my Delaware brothers seen white men near their village?'

There was no answer. Magua took out some necklaces, earrings and rings which his men had taken from the dead bodies of Englishwomen after the massacre at Fort William Henry. He gave them to the Delaware chief and his warriors.

Hard-heart became more friendly and Magua repeated his question. 'Has my brother seen strange moccasins in the forest?'

'Yes, and they have come here,' replied Hard-heart. 'The Delaware do not close their doors to any man or woman.'

'So you have "Long-rifle" with you then!' said Magua.

All the Delawares looked surprised to hear that this well-known enemy of France was in their camp. They called a meeting at their council hut and three old chiefs came to lead it. The oldest of these was the Great Chief Tamenund. Then from the hut in the middle of the village, the Munro sisters, Heyward, and Hawk-eye were brought out.

'Which of them is "Long-rifle"?' asked a chief.

'I am,' said Heyward, but Magua pointed at Hawk-eye.

Chief Tamenund asked, 'What brings a Huron to our camp?'

'I come to take back what is mine,' replied Magua.

Cora now turned to Tamenund and asked: 'Is Tamenund a father?'

Tamenund smiled a great smile, 'Of a whole tribe.'

'I ask nothing for myself. My mother's great-grandparents lived through hard times, like your people,' continued Cora. 'But please, as a father, send my sister back to her father, who is old and sick, and who misses his daughter greatly.'

'White men think that all the land is theirs,' replied Tamenund. 'They think that Indians are less than dogs. They prefer their women to be white like the snow. But I say their time here will end one day, as winter changes to spring.'

'What you say is true,' replied Cora. 'But wait. You have not heard the words of the last of your prisoners, one of your own tribe. Let him come and speak to you before you agree to give Magua what he asks for.'

'Bring this man before us,' ordered Tamenund.

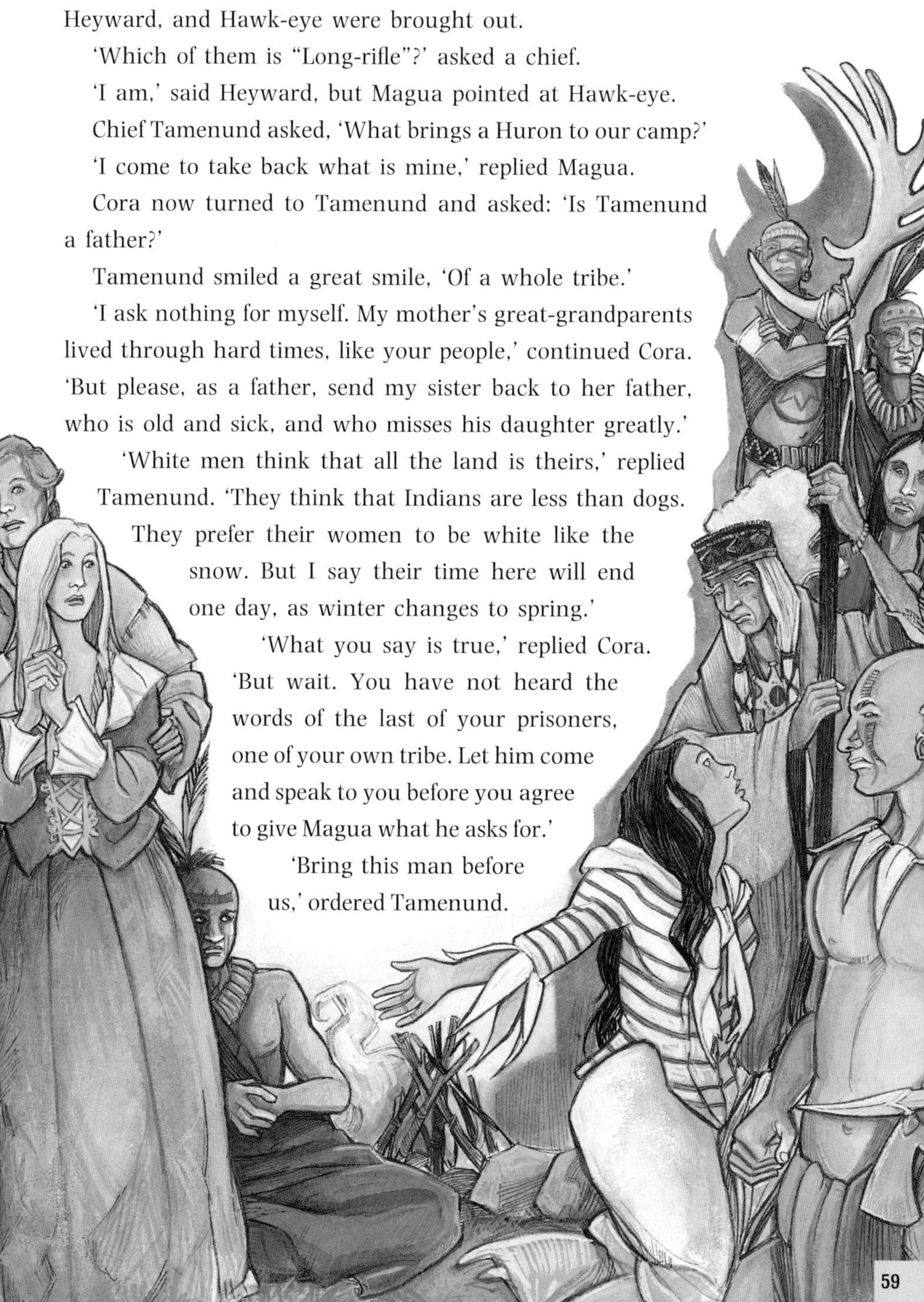

READING CHECK

Choose the correct words to complete these sentences.

a The Hurons don't kill Gamut because they think that he is a fool / magic / evil .

b The father of the sick woman / The village medicine man / Magua tells the Hurons in the council hut how someone hit him on the head.

c When the Hurons go to the caves, they find the sick woman there is now well / dead / gone.

d Magua tells the Hurons to kill Heyward / Hawk-eye / Uncas .

e Magua and the Hurons prepare to fight the Delawares / English / French .

f One of the Hurons asks his totem animal, the moose / beaver / bear , to help him when he goes to speak to the Delawares.

g Cora asks chief Tamenund to let Heyward / Uncas / Gamut speak to the Delaware tribe.

WORD WORK

Find words in the tomahawk to complete the sentences.

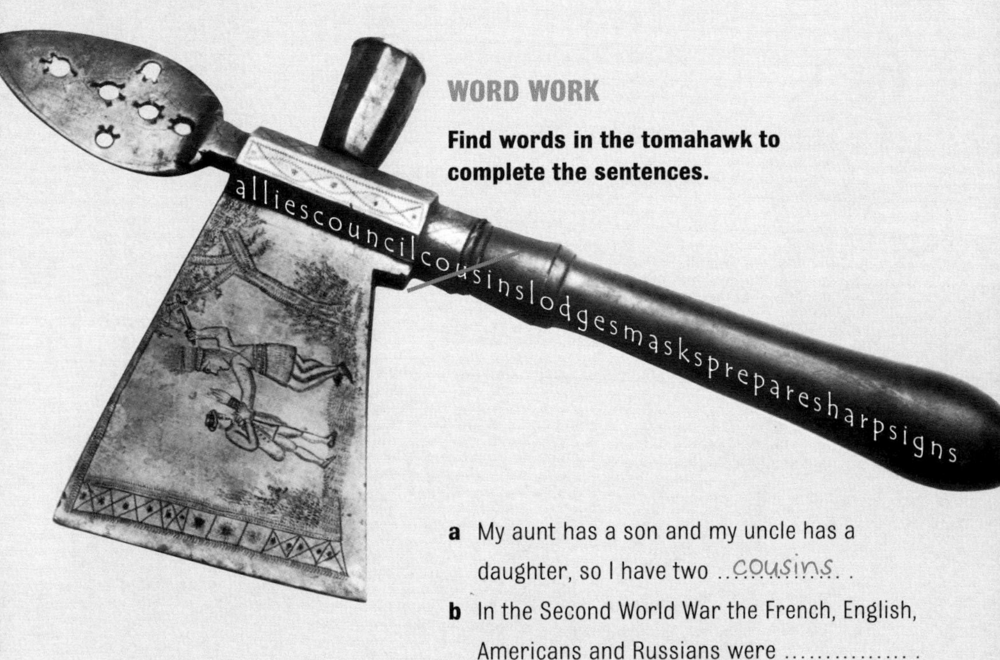

a My aunt has a son and my uncle has a daughter, so I have two ..cousins.. .

b In the Second World War the French, English, Americans and Russians were ....

c Some Indian wise men wear animal .... to cover their faces.

d Beavers' homes are called ....

e 'Be careful! That knife is .... and you could cut yourself with it.'

f The group of people who meet, talk together, and decide what happens in a town is called the town ....

g It's always good to .... for things before they happen.

h People who can't hear make .... with their hands to talk together.

GUESS WHAT

Who dies in the last chapter? Tick three pictures.

a ☐ Alice

b ☐ Cora

c ☐ Munro

d ☐ Heyward

e ☐ Hawk-eye

f ☐ Uncas

g ☐ Chingachgook

h ☐ Magua

CHAPTER 10

TO THE HAPPY HUNTING GROUND

Uncas was brought out of the prison hut and taken to the great chief Tamenund. The whole Delaware tribe stood in a big circle watching him.

'What language do you speak?' asked Tamenund.

'Delaware, like my father and his father,' answered Uncas.

'Why do you crawl like a **snake** into the Delaware camp?'

Another chief spoke. 'He is a dog that follows English paths.'

'And you are dogs that eat French food,' replied Uncas, looking grimly around him. Many warriors jumped up at these words, but Tamenund made a sign to stay calm.

'Delaware,' he continued. 'A warrior who leaves his tribe – and leaves it during hard times – is an evil man twice over. My children, he is yours.'

Many of the warriors ran forward to throw Uncas into the great fire that burned nearby. Heyward tried to go to his friend, Hawk-eye looked grim, and Cora threw herself at Tamenund's feet, asking him to save Uncas's life.

The Mohican stayed calm, even when a Delaware warrior pulled off his shirt. But immediately the Delaware stared at Uncas's chest, and pointed to the blue tortoise on it.

'Who are you?' asked Tamenund.

'Uncas, jumping deer, son of Chingachgook, the great snake.'

'I had a friend called Uncas when I was young. He was a great chief,' said Tamenund.

'I am the great-grandson of that man,' explained Uncas. 'But all the Mohicans are dead now, except me and my father.'

'It is true,' said Tamenund. 'Our wise men told us many stories of Mohicans in English lands, and now at last you have

snake a long thin animal with no legs

come home to our council hut.'

Uncas now went and cut the ropes round Hawk-eye's wrists with his own knife. Then he led the scout to Tamenund.

'Great Father,' he said. 'This man is a good friend.'

'But he is "Long-rifle" who has killed so many of our kind.'

'Hurons, yes, but never Delawares,' said Hawk-eye.

'If I am welcome here,' said Uncas, 'so is my friend.'

'Where is the Huron who told me so many lies?' asked Tamenund.

Magua stood up. 'You will not keep what is mine,' he said.

Tamenund turned to Uncas. 'Tell me, my son, do you and Hawk-eye belong to this man?'

'No, my father. I was caught by a trick.'

'And what of the white man and the pale woman he cares for?' asked Tamenund.

'They should travel on an open path. She was rescued fairly.'

'And the woman Magua left here, is she his?'

Uncas said nothing, but turned away sadly.

'My son is silent.'

'It is true,' said Uncas in a low voice.

Then Tamenund turned to Magua. 'Go, Huron!' he said.

'With empty hands? Or with the woman I brought here as my wife?'

Tamenund looked at Cora.

'What do you wish? He is a brave warrior, and a great chief of his people. Will you go with him? Will you have his children?'

'No, I would prefer to die than to go with him.'

'Magua, she refuses. Your hut will not be a happy place.'

'Is Tamenund honest? Will he give Magua what he brought here?' asked the Huron.

'Go, then,' said Tamenund. 'Take what is yours.'

Magua took Cora by the wrist and began to **drag** her after him. The Delawares stood back to let him pass.

drag to pull strongly

revenge when you do something bad to someone because they did something bad to you

'Wait!' cried Heyward. 'Leave her and take instead gold, silver, bullets, rifles – all that you need to be a great chief.'

'Magua is strong,' cried the Huron, shaking Cora by the wrist. 'This is his **revenge** on Munro.'

'One moment there!' cried Hawk-eye. 'Take me instead of the girl, and you can have my rifle "Kill-deer" too!'

Magua seemed almost persuaded to accept what Hawk-eye offered, but, looking again at Cora, he said: 'Magua's plans do not change so easily.'

Then Uncas spoke: 'Tamenund's word is the law. The sun is in the tree branches, Huron, and you are free to go now with the woman. But when the sun is above the trees, there will be men on your tracks.'

Magua laughed at Uncas's words and, turning his back, dragged Cora out of the Delaware's camp and back towards his own village. The Delawares watched them go grimly.

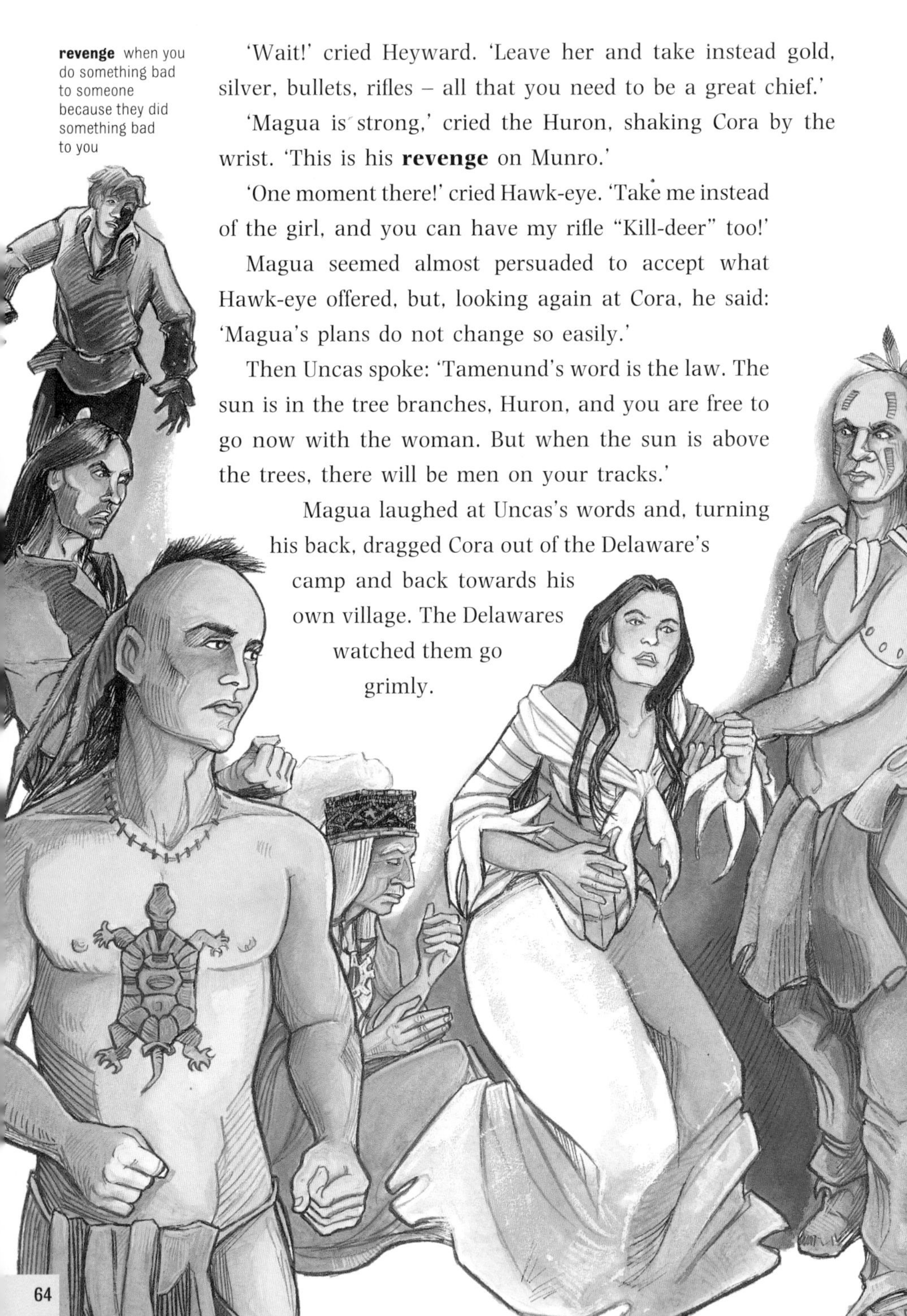

Once Magua and Cora had disappeared, the Delaware camp became very busy indeed. Uncas put on war paint and led the other Delaware men in a war dance. Fighter after fighter came to join the dance until all the warriors in the camp were there. When at last the sun reached above the trees, and the time of the truce with Magua was over, all the Delaware men were ready to follow the Mohican in his attack on the Hurons.

While Tamenund said goodbye to Uncas and his followers, Heyward and Hawk-eye left Alice in a safe place in the Delaware camp, with the women and children. Then, with Heyward and Hawk-eye at Uncas's side, two hundred Delaware fighters made their way into the forest, where they attacked the Huron gunmen they found hiding there. Most of the Hurons ran off when they realized that their hiding place had been discovered.

After that, Uncas and the Delawares had a quick war council. Uncas divided his men into different groups under different chiefs. Hawk-eye was given a group to command, and Heyward chose to fight by the scout's side. Then the war council discussed the best way to go on. Uncas wanted to **advance** quickly, but the other chiefs were against hurrying.

The meeting was interrupted when the Delawares noticed a man walking from the forest towards them. He seemed to be a Huron scout who had been sent to make peace.

'Kill him,' said Uncas to Hawk-eye.

The scout lifted 'Kill-deer' to his eye, and then let his rifle fall again, and laughed. 'It's the singing teacher.'

Hawk-eye put down his rifle and crawled through the bushes until he was close to the man. There he sang a few notes of an English hymn, to tell Gamut that he was among friends. After that, he stepped out from behind the bushes and brought the singing teacher back to speak to the war council.

'The Hurons, with Magua at their head, are hiding in great numbers deep in the forest,' Gamut explained when Hawk-eye questioned him. 'And Cora is a prisoner in the cave.'

advance to move forward

'The cave! Then we must rescue her at once!' cried Heyward.

Uncas looked at Hawk-eye.

'Give me twenty men,' said the scout, 'and I'll go to the right, along by the stream and past the beavers' lake. We'll get Munro and Chingachgook from the beavers' lodge, and then attack the Hurons on the right. At the same time you, Uncas, must attack Magua from the front. Then we'll hurry on, attack the village, and rescue Cora from the cave.'

They explained the plan to the different Delaware chiefs, and Hawk-eye led his men off. He had not gone far before he realized that the singing teacher had come with them.

'What are you doing here without a rifle?' asked Hawk-eye.

'I have my **catapult**,' said Gamut, bringing one out of his pocket. 'And I'll use that to help Cora.'

'Very well,' agreed Hawk-eye. 'You can come with us and use your catapult. But no singing, remember?'

Hawk-eye led his men along the dry bed of a river until a stream of running water crossed their path. Now, he decided, was the time to enter the forest. But as soon as Hawk-eye's men appeared above the river bank, they were met by a rain of Huron bullets killing one of their men.

'Behind the trees! Quick!' cried Hawk-eye, and they all obeyed him.

There was a long exchange of shots between the two sides. Then some Hurons moved forwards and to the left, hoping to surround the Delawares. The situation was serious for Hawk-eye's men. The trees no longer protected them.

Suddenly they heard shots from Uncas's part of the forest, and the Hurons who were attacking them turned, confused. Hawk-eye and his men immediately advanced, killing all the Hurons that they could.

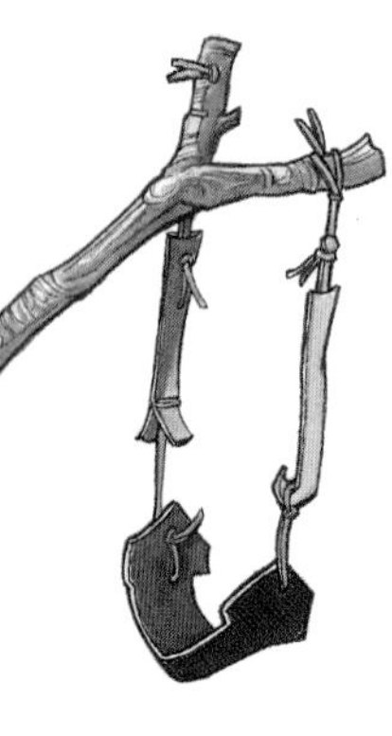

catapult a Y-shaped piece of wood with leather between the top ends; you use it to shoot stones

Soon after this, rifle shots came from Chingachgook and Munro at the beaver's lake. Shocked by this, the Hurons who were left ran off into the forest. Chingachgook and Munro joined Hawk-eye, Heyward and the rest, and they hurried to the centre of the forest to make a quick attack on the Hurons' right, while Uncas attacked from the front.

Uncas, who had seen Magua in the battle, ran forward to attack him, but the Huron chief turned and hurried away from the battlefield. So the Delawares advanced, and soon the battle reached the Huron village. There was a fierce fight in front of the council hut, and the ground was quickly covered with Huron dead. Magua now ran off with two Huron warriors towards the cave. Uncas ran after him at once, and he was followed by Hawk-eye, Heyward, and Gamut.

It was difficult for the rescuers to see as they hurried along the cave's dark passages, but suddenly a white dress appeared in the darkness.

'It's Cora,' cried Heyward, and they ran on faster than ever.

Now their path lay up a slope, and the Hurons shot back down at them. At last they could see four dark figures standing for a moment against the sky above them. Magua was escaping through a cave entrance high up on the other side of the mountain. With a growl Uncas ran out after him.

'Stop, Magua!' he called, shaking his tomahawk angrily.

Cora, Magua, and the two Hurons were now on a high rock **ledge**. They had no more bullets left.

'I will go no higher,' cried Cora as she looked down the mountain. 'Kill me if you must, but I will stop here.'

The Huron chief pulled out his knife. 'Choose, woman, my knife or my bed,' he growled.

Cora fell to her knees in front of Magua, and he lifted his knife in the air to **stab** her to death, but at that moment, with a loud cry, Uncas jumped onto the ledge in front of him. Magua stepped back, and one of the other Hurons stabbed Cora in the heart. Now Magua drove his knife into Uncas's back. Then, as the Mohican tried to stand, Magua stabbed him again and again in the chest until he fell back, dead.

ledge a flat piece of rock on the side of a mountain

stab to push a knife into someone

When Heyward and Hawk-eye reached the ledge, Magua and his two warriors had already left, and Cora and Uncas lay dead before them.

Hawk-eye, now thirsty for revenge, saw something moving higher up on the mountain and lifted his rifle to shoot. But it was only Gamut, who was dropping a large rock on one of the Hurons' heads below him. Then Magua jumped out from a narrow space between two rocks, pushing the other Huron to his death on the rocks far below. He was trying to escape by jumping across a wide empty space from one rock ledge to another. But the second ledge was too far away, and his feet didn't land on it as he had planned. Now his moccasins were touching empty air, and he held on with both hands to a mountain bush to stop himself from falling.

With a grim face the scout lifted 'Kill-deer' to his eye and shot Magua in the back. The Huron chief fell like a stone to the ground below.

The next day was black for the Delawares. They had won the war and had burnt the Huron village to the ground, but their hearts were heavy. They sang no victory songs. Instead they **mourned**. The whole tribe – men, women and children – stood in a circle in the middle of their camp.

In the centre of this circle lay the dead Cora on a bed of sweet-smelling flowers. Indian blankets covered her, and six young Delaware women moved around her in a slow dance of mourning. General Munro sat at her feet, his face full of sadness, and Gamut stood by his side. Heyward stood nearby, trying hard not to show his feelings.

Next to this first group was a second, even sadder than the first. Sitting, as in life, was the dead body of Uncas wearing feathers in his hair, necklaces, ear-rings, and the fine clothes of a Delaware chief. He almost seemed to be living, but his face was lifeless. Chingachgook stood in front of him, his face

mourn to be sad because someone has died

a grim mask that gave no sign of feeling. Hawk-eye stood nearby, and Tamenund was there, too.

As one person the whole tribe mourned the deaths of Uncas and of Cora. First they carried Cora's lifeless body up a small hill, where they put it deep in the earth between some trees. Gamut sang a sad song. After that they put Uncas deep in the earth, lying with his face to the east. They covered his body with earth and leaves, then Chingachgook spoke.

'Why do my brothers mourn? Why do my sisters cry? Uncas has gone to the happy hunting-ground. He was good and brave. The Great Spirit needed him and has called him away. I am left here alone, and my tribe has gone from the lake and the hills of the Delawares.'

'Go, now, all of you,' said Tamenund. 'I will not stay with you long. The time of the red man is finished and the earth now belongs to the palefaces. This morning I saw the sons of the tortoise strong and healthy. But now I have lived to see the last of the Mohicans.'

READING CHECK

1 Are these sentences true or false? Tick the boxes.

		True	False
a	Tamenund believes Uncas's story and decides to fight the Hurons with him.	✓	☐
b	Tamenund welcomes Hawk-eye to the Delaware village because of Uncas.	☐	☐
c	Alice and Heyward must leave the Delaware village with Magua.	☐	☐
d	Cora must leave the Delaware village with Magua.	☐	☐
e	Heyward offers to go with Magua instead of Cora.	☐	☐
f	Uncas and the Delawares put on war paint and do a war dance before Magua leaves the village.	☐	☐
g	Gamut comes from the Huron camp to join Hawk-eye and the others and fight against the French.	☐	☐
h	The Delaware warriors follow the Hurons back to their village.	☐	☐
i	Cora is a prisoner in the Huron prison hut.	☐	☐
j	Hawk-eye kills Magua with his gun.	☐	☐
k	At the end of the story there is only one Mohican alive – Chingachgook.	☐	☐

2 Complete the missing information in the chapter summary.

When the Delawares see the **(a)** tortoise on Uncas's chest, they realise that he isn't an enemy. Tamenund trusts Uncas because he knew Uncas's **(b)** .... Magua leaves the Delaware village with **(c)** ...., but Uncas promises to fight him. As the Delawares prepare to attack, they see **(d)** .... walking towards them. He tells them that Cora is a prisoner in the **(e)** .... Chingachgook and Munro join the fighting in the **(f)** ...., and they advance to the Huron village. Magua runs away up the mountain with Cora. When Magua tries to stab Cora, **(g)** .... jumps in his way. A Huron stabs Cora in the heart and Magua stabs Uncas to death. Finally Magua dies; **(h)** .... shoots him.

WORD WORK

Use the definitions of new words from Chapter 10 to complete the crossword.

1 a narrow piece of rock that sticks out on the side of a cliff or a mountain

2 a kind of long thin animal without legs that crawls along the ground

3 to move forward in a battle

4 to pull somebody or something along with difficulty

5 something that you do to punish somebody who has hurt you or done something bad to you

6 to feel great sadness because somebody has died

7 to push a knife or other pointed object into somebody or something

8 a Y-shaped stick with leather attached on each side that is used for shooting stones

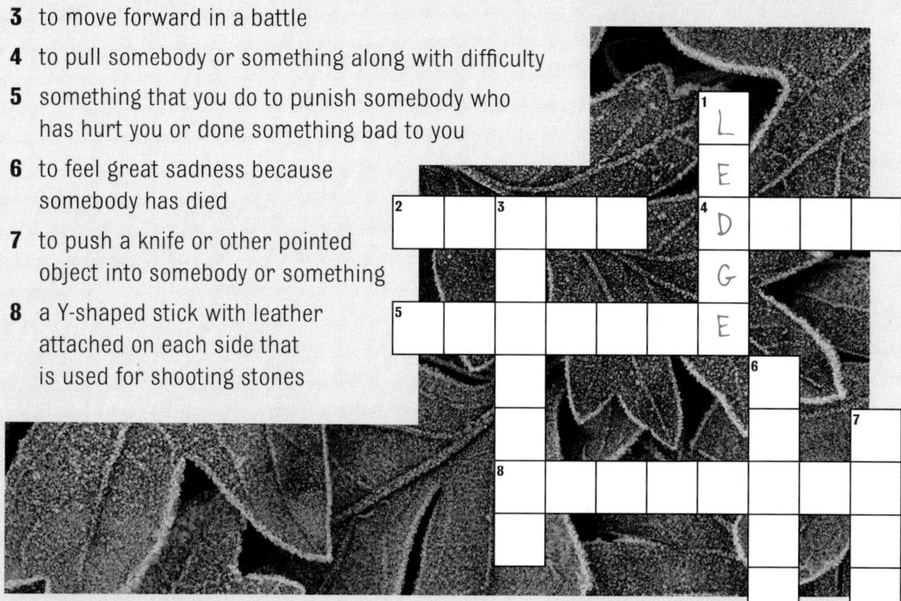

GUESS WHAT

What happens after the story ends? Choose from these ideas or add your own.

a ☐ Heyward and Alice marry and go to live in Scotland.

b ☐ General Munro goes back to Fort Edward and dies there of a broken heart.

c ☐ Hawk-eye becomes like a second son to Chingachgook.

d ☐ Gamut stays in the Delaware village and marries a Delaware woman.

e ☐ Tamenund agrees to sell his tribe's land to the French.

f ☐ ....

g ☐ ....

h ☐ ....

PROJECT A *A letter home*

1 Read Alice Munro's letter and answer the questions.

Dear Cousin,
We are in Fort William Henry, at last. We were brought here by Duncan Heyward to visit our father. We had some problems with Magua, our Indian guide, but two Mohicans – Chingachgook and his son Uncas – and their friend 'Hawk-eye' helped us. Now we spend most of our time in our room reading and writing. We don't see a lot of Duncan. He is very busy with army work. Cora and I told him that it is very bad of him not to come to see us, but he only laughs at us – of course his army work is very important.
The French army is getting nearer. I feel worried.
I will write again soon.
lots of love, Alice

a	Who is Alice writing to?	
b	Where is Alice?	
c	How did she get there?	
d	Why did she go there?	
e	Who did she have problems with?	
f	Who helped her?	
g	How does she spend her time?	
h	Why does she not see much of Duncan?	
i	What does Duncan do wrong?	
j	What's happening?	
k	How does Alice feel?	

2 Use these notes to write a letter from David Gamut.

To:	sister
Place:	Fort Edward
Brought there by:	God
Why?	to tell people in North America how to live good lives
Problems with:	Huron Indians, the allies of the French
Helped by:	General Webb's men, God
Spends most of time:	in church, singing and praying
Doesn't see:	General Webb
Why not?	busy with army work
What does he do wrong?	not go to church
What's happening?	reinforcements getting ready to leave for Fort William Henry
Feeling:	excited

3 Write a letter from Duncan Heyward to his parents.

PROJECT B *Animal beliefs*

1 American Indians believed that these animals were special. Why? Look at the pictures and complete the sentences.

AMERICAN INDIAN ANIMAL BELIEFS

a American Indians believed that a huge _ _ _ _ _ _ _ _ _ carried the world on its back.

b They believed that _ _ _ _ _ _ were magical animals

c They believed that _ _ _ _ were fast animals.

d They believed that _ _ _ _ gave fire to man and were friendly.

e They believed that _ _ _ _ were quiet and dishonest.

f They believed that _ _ _ _ _ brought death from the sky.

g They believed that _ _ _ _ _ guided people and made them strong.

2 What do you believe about these animals? Match the animals with the words to describe their characters. Use a dictionary to help you.

a owl
b fox
c black cat
d mouse
e lion
f horse

brave
clever
faithful
fast
fierce
hard-working
lucky
greedy
dirty
proud
quiet
reliable
sly
slow
strong
unreliable
unlucky
wise
obedient

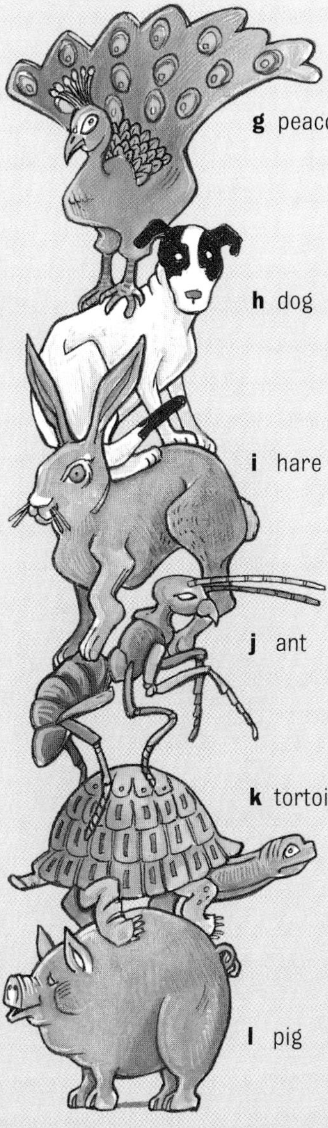

g peacock
h dog
i hare
j ant
k tortoise
l pig

3 Read the project about animal beliefs on page 76.

4 Are these beliefs the same in your country?

Cats

Cats were first brought to America from Europe in the sixteenth century. At that time, people, especially farmers, liked cats because they killed mice and rats, and today many people think that cats make good pets.

Many people in the United States and England believe that seeing a black cat will bring good luck. They think that if a black cat comes to your house you should not chase it away, because it is bringing good luck. But cats have not always been so lucky; for a long time people believed that cats were the evil friends of witches, or even the witches themselves.

Some people believe that cats know what weather is coming; they wash behind their ears when it is going to rain, and they jump around excitedly when a storm is coming.

5 Write a project about some of the animal beliefs in your country.